SPELLING

MW01127818

ENGLISH in context

Mrs. McKay

ENGLISH in context

CAPITALIZATION AND PUNCTUATION

GRAMMAR AND USAGE

READING COMPREHENSION

SPELLING

VOCABULARY

WRITING

Development and Production: Laurel Associates, Inc.
Cover Art: Elisa Ligon

SADDLEBACK PUBLISHING, INC.
Three Watson
Irvine, CA 92618-2767

E-Mail: info@sdlback.com
Website: www.sdlback.com

ISBN 1-56254-354-7

Printed in the United States of America
05 04 03 02 01 00   9 8 7 6 5 4 3 2 1

CONTENTS

INTRODUCTION

What kind of image do you want to project in the world? Accurate spelling is an important part of your "image in writing." Like a bright smile or a firm handshake, consistently correct spelling makes a positive impression and commands respect.

By following a few simple procedures, you can make a dramatic improvement in your current spelling skills.

1 Pay attention as you read.

Take a good look at difficult words so you can "see" them in your mind when you need to. Like all skills, your visual memory will improve as you continue to practice. In time there will be more words in your "memory bank" than in any computer spell-checker!

2 Take the time to master a few spelling rules.

Although there are many exceptions, the spelling of *most* English words follows predictable rules and patterns. The exercises in this book will help you become familiar with the sounds and spelling patterns of English.

3 Break long words into syllables; say the words aloud.

Listening closely to the different sounds in a word can help you figure out how to spell it. Spelling a long word part by part is easier than attacking the word as a whole.

4 Write out difficult words four or five times.

Monitor your handwriting as you practice spelling a word. Careless letter formation is often seen as an error in spelling. Legible handwriting shows respect for your reader and will also improve your grades.

5 Proofread, proofread, proofread.

Never consider your writing "finished" until you've carefully read it over for errors. The time it takes to correct your mistakes—and rewrite, if necessary—will pay off every time.

6 Cultivate the "dictionary habit."

"Guesswork" always results in needless spelling errors. It only makes sense to keep a dictionary handy. Why take a chance when you need only a moment to be *certain* of how a word is spelled?

7 Keep a list of your personal spelling demons.

Each of us has his or her own "spelling demons"—certain words that trip us up every time we use them. Experts recommend recording these words and keeping the list handy for quick reference. A form for this purpose is provided on page 102 of this book.

FOUNDATIONS OF SPELLING
FOR HELP WITH THIS UNIT, SEE THE SPELLING REFERENCE GUIDE, RULES 1–10.

UNIT
1

1 — LEGIBLE HANDWRITING

There are 26 letters in the English alphabet. Every English word is made up of one or more of these letters. It is important to form each letter correctly. Why? Sloppy handwriting often looks like careless spelling.

A

Write each capital and lowercase letter as perfectly as you can.

Aa _____	*Hh* _____	*Oo* _____	*Uu* _____
Bb _____	*Ii* _____	*Pp* _____	*Vv* _____
Cc _____	*Jj* _____	*Qq* _____	*Ww* _____
Dd _____	*Kk* _____	*Rr* _____	*Xx* _____
Ee _____	*Ll* _____	*Ss* _____	*Yy* _____
Ff _____	*Mm* _____	*Tt* _____	*Zz* _____
Gg _____	*Nn* _____		

B

**Can you form all the letters clearly and connect them correctly?
Is your usual handwriting too big or too small? Practice writing the
words below in your best cursive handwriting.**

youth _____   flatter _____

mountain _____   bread _____

friendly _____   kindness _____

C

Practice writing the names of these interesting people and places. Be sure to space your letters evenly.

1. Michael Jordan

_____

2. Walla Walla, Washington

_____

3. Barbra Streisand

_____

4. Albuquerque, New Mexico

_____

5. Yosemite National Park

_____

6. Ernest Hemingway

_____

7. Pike's Peak

_____

8. Abigail Adams

_____

9. Niagara Falls

_____

10. Tara Lipinsky

_____

D

Read the tongue twister silently. Then write it out neatly on the lines below.

Betty bought a bit of butter.
But, she said, this butter's bitter.
If I'd bought a bit of better butter
it would have made my batter better.

TRY IT OUT!
Read the tongue twister aloud as fast as you can.

_____

_____

_____

_____

2 — ALPHABETICAL ORDER

The customary order of letters in any language is alphabetical. Alphabetical order in English begins with **A** and ends with **Z**.

A B C D E F G H I J K L M N O P Q R S T U V W X Y Z

Words in the dictionary are arranged alphabetically. To quickly find the word you want, you must be thoroughly familiar with alphabetical order.

A

Write the letter of the alphabet that comes just before and just after each letter below.

1. ___ P ___
2. ___ O ___
3. ___ I ___
4. ___ G ___
5. ___ N ___
6. ___ D ___
7. ___ Y ___
8. ___ E ___
9. ___ K ___

B

Number the words in each list to show alphabetical order.

1. ___ crowd
   ___ friend
   ___ neighbor

2. ___ idle
   ___ false
   ___ jolly

3. ___ success
   ___ vicious
   ___ permanent

C

First letters do not always show alphabetical order. Read the word lists below. Use the *second* or *third* letter in each word to decide which word comes first. Then write numbers to alphabetize the words in each list.

1. ___ useful
   ___ unhappy
   ___ usually

2. ___ plentiful
   ___ plight
   ___ plum

3. ___ tremendous
   ___ translation
   ___ tournament

USING A DICTIONARY 3

People with good spelling skills also have good dictionary skills.

A

Notice the different kinds of information in the dictionary entry below.

ac•quaint•ance (ə kwānt´ ns) **n. 1.** knowledge of a thing or person gotten from one's own experience [I have some *acquaintance* with modern art.] **2.** a person one knows but not as a close friend [My sister is an *acquaintance* of your brother.]

LOOK IT UP!

How can you look up a word you can't spell? If you know the first two or three letters, you won't have trouble finding it. Remember that most words are spelled the way they sound!

Use information in the dictionary entry to answer the questions.

1. How many syllables are in the word *acquaintance*? _____

2. The accent mark (´) shows that which syllable is stressed in pronunciation? _____

3. Which part of speech is the word *acquaintance*? _____

4. How many meanings are given? _____

5. Write a sentence in which you use the word *acquaintance*.

_____

B

Read the statements below. Write *T* if the statement is true and *F* if the statement is false.

1. ____ Knowing alphabetical order is an important dictionary skill.

2. ____ A dictionary entry defines a word but does not show you how the word is used.

3. ____ The dictionary entry on this page would be found at the front of the book.

4. ____ Dividing a word into syllables will never help you spell the word.

4 — PRONOUNCING CONSONANTS AND VOWELS

All the letters of the alphabet are symbols for sounds. There are two major groups of letter sounds in English. These two groups are called *consonants* and *vowels*.

VOWELS — a, e, i, o, u, and sometimes **y**

Vowels are *open* mouth sounds. You make vowel sounds with an open flow of breath.

CONSONANTS — b, c, d, f, g, h, j, k, l, m, n, p, q, r, s, t, v, w, x, y, z

Consonants are *closed* mouth sounds. You make these sounds by blocking your breath with your teeth, lips, or tongue.

A

Pay attention to the consonant sound as you read the practice words aloud. Then circle the word that correctly completes the sentence.

	SOUND	PRACTICE WORDS	
1.	d	dad, bed	To make this sound I block my breath with my (tongue / lips).
2.	b	baby, sob	To make this sound I block my breath with my (teeth / lips).
3.	f	fun, awful	I use my bottom lip and my (tongue / teeth) to make this sound.
4.	k	kick, bike	I make this sound in the (front / back) of my mouth.
5.	v	van, oven	I make this sound in the (front / back) of my mouth.
6.	l	lip, pal	I could not make this sound without using my (tongue / lips).
7.	w	wish, wet	I could not make this sound without using my (lips / teeth).
8.	p	pen, wipe	When I make this sound my breath goes (out / in).

Q. Why is it important to learn letter sounds?

CHOMP

Ribbit...

A. Because **most** words in English are spelled the way they sound.

10

B

Write a letter from the box to correctly complete each statement.

h	m	r	s	t

1. To pronounce the letter ____, I place my tongue just behind my top teeth.

2. I let out a quick puff of air to make the letter ____.

3. My lips are closed when I pronounce the letter ____.

4. I make the sound of ____ in the back of my mouth.

5. When I pronounce the letter ____, my tongue touches my bottom teeth.

C

Listen carefully as you say the words aloud. Circle two words in each group that have the same *vowel sound*.

1. ball   hand   bell   mad

2. desk   task   cent   deed

3. hid   hall   hide   did

4. plate   great   pleat   plan

5. kite   crisp   might   brief

6. hoop   got   sock   hope

7. fan   fun   top   pup

8. toy   try   two   spy

9. mutt   push   flute   strut

10. home   come   prove   roam

11

All the letters in the alphabet are either consonants or vowels. The vowels are **a**, **e**, **i**, **o**, and **u**. The letter **y** can be either a consonant or a vowel depending on the sound it makes. All the other letters are consonants. In most English words, a consonant makes its own sound.

A

Next to each word listed below, write two more words that begin with the same consonant.

1. **b**ed _____ _____

2. **c**ap _____ _____

3. **d**ot _____ _____

B

Now add consonants to complete the words in each category.

1. ___lum   o___ange   g___ape

   peac___   ___anana   water___elon

   app___e   a___ricot   ___ineapple

2. ___omato   s___inach   carro___

   o___ion   bee___   ce___ery

   cor___   lettu___e   ___ea

C

Write your full name on the line. Then tell how many consonants are in your name.

name: _____

number of consonants: _____

12

CONSONANT CLUSTERS 6

Many sounds are made by combining two or more consonants. These letter combinations are called *consonant clusters*. Study the examples.

SPELLING	SOUND	EXAMPLES
sh	**sh**	**sh**op, **sh**irt, pu**sh**
sp	**sp**	**sp**ell, **sp**ark, wa**sp**
ch/tch	**ch**	ma**tch**, pi**tch**, **ch**urch
wh	**hw/h**	**wh**at, **wh**isper, **wh**ole

In most consonant clusters the spelling and the sound are the same. But watch out for exceptions. *Some sounds may be spelled in different ways!*

A

Use one of the consonant clusters above to complete the words in each list.

1. ___ ___ eep

   ___ ___ ark

   ___ ___ adow.

2. ___ ___ en

   ___ ___ eat

   ___ ___ om

3. pa ___ ___ ___

   fe ___ ___ ___

   la ___ ___ ___

B

Complete the sentences by filling in the blanks with consonant clusters.

1. In ___ ___ ich year did Eli ___ ___ itney invent the cotton gin?

2. The three-part leaves of a ___ ___ amrock are a bright ___ ___ ade of green.

3. ___ ___ y did Captain Ahab hunt the ___ ___ ite ___ ___ ale named Moby Dick?

4. A ___ ___ ace ___ ___ uttle can laun ___ ___ satellites ___ ___ ile orbiting the earth.

SHORT AND LONG VOWEL SOUNDS

Every vowel has at least two sounds. Read the example words aloud. Listen to the difference between the *short* vowel sounds and the *long* vowel sounds.

	SHORT VOWEL SOUNDS	LONG VOWEL SOUNDS
a	plan	plane
e	bet	be
i	rip	ripe
o	got	go
u	us	use

A

Read the names. Decide which kind of sound the *boldfaced* vowel makes. Write *L* for *long* or *S* for *short* on the line. Hint: If you need help, look at the example words.

1. ____ H**a**nnah   5. ____ C**i**ndy   9. ____ **A**my

2. ____ S**u**san   6. ____ J**o**anne   10. ____ B**u**d

3. ____ **E**ddie   7. ____ Br**a**d   11. ____ M**i**chael

4. ____ T**o**m   8. ____ P**e**te   12. ____ K**i**m

The letter **y** can be either a vowel or a consonant.

In some words the letter **y** is a vowel because it *sounds* like a vowel. In other words, **y** has a consonant sound.

EXAMPLES:

my   The *y* has the *long i* sound.
stud**y**   The *y* has the *long e* sound.
yet   The *y* has the *consonant* sound.

B

young	fry
canyon	happy
money	truly
beyond	key
yellow	rely
myself	apply

Read the words in the box aloud. Listen for the sound the *y* makes. Then write each word in the correct column.

LONG E SOUND	LONG I SOUND	CONSONANT SOUND
_____	_____	_____
_____	_____	_____
_____	_____	_____
_____	_____	_____

C

Show what you know about consonants and vowels. Circle the state name that correctly completes each sentence.

1. (Oklahoma / Oregon) begins with the long *o* sound.

2. (Arkansas / Arizona) begins with a vowel and ends with a consonant.

3. (Indiana / Idaho) begins with the long *i* sound.

4. (Ohio / Alabama) begins and ends with the same long vowel sound.

5. (Hawaii / California) ends with three vowels in a row.

6. (Maine / Vermont) begins and ends with a consonant.

D

Read the sentences about the state of Wyoming. Notice the words with a *boldfaced* letter. Decide whether the boldfaced vowel in each word is *short* or *long*. Then write the words in the correct column.

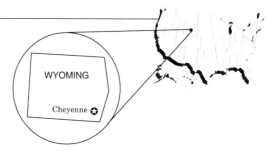

WYOMING

Cheyenne

1. W**y**oming is a b**i**g st**a**te in the W**e**st Central region.

SHORT VOWELS	LONG VOWELS
_____	_____
_____	_____

2. Wyoming h**a**s a smaller popul**a**tion th**a**n an**y** other state.

SHORT VOWELS	LONG VOWELS
_____	_____
_____	_____

8 — MISPRONOUNCED WORDS

If you don't *say* a word correctly, the chances are you won't spell it correctly, either. Sometimes people talk too fast and skip over one or more sounds in a word. And sometimes people *add* sounds that don't belong.

EXAMPLES: **SKIPPING A SOUND**   **ADDING A SOUND**

pro**babl**y, not pro**bal**y   **ath**lete, not **atha**lete

A

Circle the correct spelling. Then write the sentence on the writing lines.

A good speller is a good listener. By paying attention to the *sounds* in a word, you can often figure out how to spell it.

1. Tea and hot (chocolate / choclate) were the preferred
   (bevrages / beverages) 200 years ago.

   _____

   _____

2. Most Americans say that their (favrite / favorite)
   (vegetable / vegtable) is corn.

   _____

   _____

3. To stay healthy and maintain their (strength / strenth), adults
   are (supposed / sposed) to drink two quarts of water a day.

   _____

   _____

4. Sugar didn't reach Europe in (quanity / quantity) until
   the (twelf / twelfth) century.

   _____

   _____

If you're not sure how to pronounce or spell a word, try breaking it up into *syllables*. (A syllable is one or more letters that make a single sound.) Then count the syllables and say or spell the word one part at a time.

EXAMPLE: priv/i/lege = 3 syllables,
3 separate sounds

TRY IT OUT!

Say *privilege* aloud. Did you pronounce the second syllable distinctly?

The words below are commonly mispronounced and misspelled. On the line, use slashes (/ /) to divide each word into syllables.

1. sophomore _____

2. temperament _____

3. mathematics _____

4. environment _____

The clues below are common misspellings of words that are frequently mispronounced. Solve the puzzle by spelling the words correctly.

ACROSS
  2. grievious
  4. liberry
  6. ordnary
  7. burgular

DOWN
  1. disasterous
  3. camra
  5. boundry

9 — MORE MISPRONOUNCED WORDS

Remember to *listen to the sounds* as you say the words out loud. If you're still not sure, try breaking the words into syllables. And there's always the dictionary—check it out!

A

Circle the correctly spelled word in each group.

1. reckonize   recagnize   recognize   recanize

2. government   guverment   goverment   govverment

3. represent   repersent   reprosent   reppresent

4. accidentlly   accidently   accidentally   accedentelly

5. grandmother   granmother   grannmother   granddmother

B

Underline the correctly spelled words to complete the sentences. Then write the paragraph on the lines.

Our class went on an (intersting / intresting / interesting) field trip in (February / Febyewary / Febuary). The zookeeper (suprized / surprised / supprised) us with some (especially / expecially / espeshally) exciting news. We were (jest / just / jist) thrilled to see (sevral / several / sevrel) newborn gorillas! If you could see the (pictures / pitchers) we took, you would see for (yourselves / yourselfs) how (hansome / handsome / handsum) they are.

_____

_____

_____

_____

_____

_____

Many spelling errors are made by *transposing*, or reversing, the letters in a word. This problem is usually caused either by carelessness or a habit of mispronunciation.

EXAMPLES: p**re**scribe, *not* p**er**scribe

              fr**ie**nd, *not* fr**ei**nd

Read the sentences. Cross out the words with transposed letters.

1. Some eagle nests (wiegh / weigh) as much as a ton.

2. (Prehaps / Perhaps) you didn't know that eagles keep the same nest throughout their lives.

3. The albatross is the (only / olny) seabird that can fly six days without moving its wings.

4. The albatross can (perform / preform) an even more amazing feat.

5. After leaving the island of its (brith / birth), it may not touch land again for (tow / two) years!

6. In a race with (sevreal / several) other speedy fish, the sailfish will finish (frist / first).

7. Moving at (olny / only) 40 miles per hour, the shark would finish a distant (thrid / third).

8. Did you know that dogs (prespire / perspire) through (their / thier) mouths?

11 — HOMOPHONES

Homophones are "sound alike" words that have different meanings and spellings. It's a good idea to memorize any homophones that cause you trouble. How can you be *certain* that you're using the word you want? Look it up in the dictionary!

EXAMPLE: **pain** (a feeling of hurting)

pane (the glass in a window)

A

Write a homophone (word that sounds exactly the same) next to each word below. The first one has been done for you.

1. aunt _____*ant*_____

2. be _____

3. bare _____

4. scent _____

5. clothes _____

6. creek _____

7. fare _____

8. flu _____

9. fowl _____

10. haul _____

11. hear _____

12. higher _____

13. maid _____

14. meat _____

B

Circle the homophone(s) that correctly complete(s) each sentence.

1. Do you prefer (plane / plain) or fancy donuts (for / four) breakfast?

2. She thinks the (rose / rows) is the prettiest (flour / flower) of all.

3. (Eye / I) wonder (weather / whether) or not the (whether / weather) will be good for skiing.

4. Have (ewe / you) (seen / scene) the (presents / presence) I got for my birthday?

5. Is that a (hole / whole) in (your / yore) new jacket?

6. The teacher (tolled / told) me that I (missed / mist) three questions on the test.

7. She could hardly (weight / wait) to show her mother the fine (seam / seem) she had (sown / sewn).

8. (Wee / We) drove (through / threw) the tunnel under the street.

9. Is that a (real / reel) diamond (in / inn) your ring?

Use homophones from Part B to complete the crossword puzzle.

ACROSS

3. line formed when two pieces of material are sewn together

5. long ago; *in days of ___*

6. in one side and out the other

7. in favor of; *to fight ___ freedom*

9. heaviness; *Her ___ is 120 pounds.*

11. aircraft; *The pilot landed the ___ smoothly.*

DOWN

1. fine powder made by grinding wheat

2. outside conditions such as temperature, rainfall, etc.

4. large mass of tiny water droplets in the air; thinner than fog.

6. rang out; said of a bell

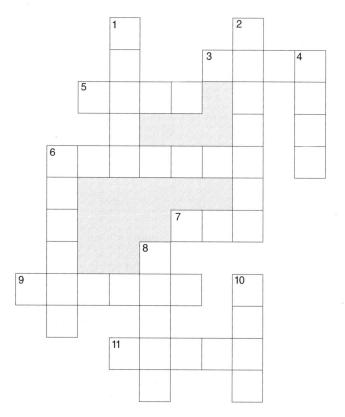

8. all of something in one piece

10. spool for winding fishing line

D

Use *both* homophones in the same sentence.

billed (sent a bill)
build (construct)   1. _____

_____

ceiling (top of a room)
sealing (closing)   2. _____

_____

cheap (inexpensive)
cheep (bird call)   3. _____

_____

feat (accomplishment)
feet (plural of foot)   4. _____

_____

groan (moan)
grown (cultivated)   5. _____

_____

heal (make well)
heel (bottom of foot)   6. _____

_____

hoarse (husky voice)
horse (animal)   7. _____

_____

mail (send by post)
male (masculine)   8. _____

_____

Some words are *misused* more than they are misspelled. Do you have trouble distinguishing any of the word pairs on this page? Add them to your personal list of spelling words at the back of this book.

A

Complete each sentence with the correct word or words.

1. (**already / all ready**) Oh, no! I'm _____ late for my appointment.

2. (**led / lead**) Mr. Gomez _____ the scouts on a nature hike.

3. (**all together / altogether**) There are _____ too many students in this small room.

4. (**already / all ready**) The chef's pies are _____ to go in the oven.

5. (**led / lead**) The music teacher will _____ the choir in the state competition.

6. (**all together / altogether**) When our group is _____ we will board the bus.

7. (**then / than**) First we will have lunch, and _____ we will go to the movie.

8. (**affect / effect**) The blizzard had a devastating _____ on our town.

9. (**then / than**) Jamal is a lot taller _____ his older brother.

10. (**affect / effect**) Bright lights _____ the pupils of your eyes.

B

Contractions and possessive pronouns are frequently confused.
Circle the correct words.

1. (They're / Their) redecorating (they're / their) apartment.

2. (Its / It's) a shame that the dog injured (its / it's) tail.

3. (Whose / Who's) purse is under (you're / your) desk?

4. Is the owner the girl (whose / who's) absent today?

A List the names of the American presidents in *alphabetical order*.

Jefferson   **Madison**   **Grant**   **Ford**

1. _____   3. _____

2. _____   4. _____

B Read the words aloud. Next to each word write **long** or **short** to tell which kind of *vowel sound* you hear.

1. fry   _____   4. friend   _____

2. tree   _____   5. you   _____

3. wrist   _____   6. buckle   _____

C Draw lines to connect *rhyming words*.

1. plate   a. tune

2. has   b. loose

3. juice   c. jazz

4. soon   d. great

D For each vowel, write an example word in each column.

	SHORT VOWEL	LONG VOWEL
1. **a**	_____	_____
2. **e**	_____	_____
3. **i**	_____	_____
4. **o**	_____	_____
5. **u**	_____	_____

E Circle the word in each pair that contains a consonant cluster.

ache / ace   bead / bread   faith / fate   clamp / camp

F Which misspellings below contain transposed letters? Underline three words.

shugar   offten   fued   wrinkel   tradgedy   porportion

G Which misspellings below are the probable result of mispronunciation? Circle three words.

potatos   diffrent   editer   paticular   hunderd   truely

H Write a pair of homophones to match each pair of clues.

1. a female deer _____   5. sunbeams _____

2. bread before baking _____   6. to lift up _____

3. a blood vessel _____   7. corridor _____

4. conceited _____   8. tote a load _____

I Notice the **boldfaced** words. On the line after each sentence, write the word that the writer intended to use.

1. She hasn't met our school's new **principle**. _____

2. Thanks for the flattering **complement**. _____

3. Cherry pie is Malcolm's favorite **desert**. _____

4. My **personnel** opinion is different from yours. _____

SPELLING PATTERNS

FOR HELP WITH THIS UNIT, SEE THE SPELLING REFERENCE GUIDE, RULES 11–25.

UNIT 2

 PREFIXES: *un, in, il, im, ir*

A *prefix* is a group of letters added at the beginning of a word. Prefixes are used to change a word's meaning. The prefixes *un, in, il, im,* and *ir* all mean **not**.

EXAMPLES: **un** + familiar = **un**familiar
im + perfect = **im**perfect

 A

Circle the correctly spelled word in each group.

1. irreplaceable   imreplaceable   ilreplaceable

2. unnumerable   innumerable   imnumerable

3. ilmature   unmature   immature

4. irlogical   illogical   unlogical

5. immortal   unmortal   ilmortal

B

Fill in the blanks with *un, in, il, im,* or *ir.*

1. ___ ___ reliable   6. ___ ___ reversible

2. ___ ___ regular   7. ___ ___ effective

3. ___ ___ legal   8. ___ ___ rehearsed

4. ___ ___ accurate   9. ___ ___ polite

5. ___ ___ possible   10. ___ ___ contested

PREFIXES: *re, de, dis, mis, inter, sub* 14

Study the six common prefixes and their meanings.

PREFIX	MEANING	EXAMPLES
de	off, away from	**de**form, **de**grade
dis	away from, out of	**dis**charge, **dis**agree
inter	among, between	**inter**weave, **inter**act
mis	wrong, wrongly	**mis**placed, **mis**understood
re	again, back	**re**attach, **re**compute
sub	under, less than	**sub**conscious, **sub**merge

Use prefixes from the box to complete the words.

1. His ___ ___ ___ability did not prevent him from attending
   the ___ ___ ___ ___ ___national conference.

2. Can you ___ ___upholster the seats in my ___ ___ ___compact car?

3. It would be a ___ ___ ___courtesy to be late for my job
   ___ ___ ___ ___ ___view.

4. I was ___ ___ ___informed about how much
   it would cost to ___ ___bug my computer.

Hello. I'm baaack!

5. Since her work is ___ ___ ___standard, she
   will have to ___ ___focus her efforts.

6. He ___ ___ ___placed the instructions for
   ___ ___frosting the old refrigerator.

7. The children ___ ___ ___obeyed their mother
   by ___ ___ ___behaving in the store.

8. Perhaps the fortune teller ___ ___ ___calculated
   when the ghost would ___ ___appear.

27

PREFIXES: *per, pre, pro*

The prefixes *per, pro,* and *pre* are often confused.

PREFIX	MEANING	EXAMPLES
per	throughout, thoroughly	**per**sist, **per**vade
pre	before, ahead	**pre**fix, **pre**heat
pro	forward, favoring	**pro**ject, **pro**gress

A

Fill in the blanks with *per, pro,* or *pre*. Write the completed words on the lines.

1. The wedding ___ ___ ___ cession moved slowly down the aisle.

2. All expectant mothers need ___ ___ ___ natal care.

3. Factory work gives you a new ___ ___ ___ spective on labor problems.

4. Fossils tell us what creatures lived in ___ ___ ___ historic times.

B

Find spelling errors in only six words. Write *all* the words on the lines. Then circle each word in the hidden words puzzle. Puzzle words may go in *any* direction. Check off each word as you find it.

```
P P R E D I C T D A S
R E H I N G T R H P R
O N R O E U E G H R N
P O T S T V C H E O S
O I N W E N I R I C E
S S P S R C D T S L D
E S R G P T U Y P A A
L E D T S A J T G I U
P F A N C D E H E M S
A O V E S L R V S A R
G R R D L E P O R P E
T P E R T U R B T H P
```

___ 1. precaution _____

___ 2. presecute _____

___ 3. proclaim _____

___ 4. prejudice _____

___ 5. perfession _____

___ 6. preturb _____

___ 7. persevere _____

___ 8. prepose _____

___ 9. propel _____

___ 10. perdict _____

___ 11. persuade _____

___ 12. pertend _____

28

The suffix *ly* turns an adjective into an adverb.

quiet + **ly** = **quietly**   entire + **ly** = **entirely**

For some adjectives, however, you must do more than just add *ly*:

If an adjective ends in *le*, drop the *e* and just add *y*:

sensibl~~e~~ + **ly** = **sensibly**
probabl~~e~~ + **ly** = **probably**

If an adjective ends in *y*, change the *y* to *i* before adding the suffix:

merr~~y~~ + **i** + **ly** = **merrily**

If an adjective ends in *c*, add *al* before adding *ly*:

comic + **al** + **ly** = **comically**

Read the sentences. Then rewrite the boldfaced adjectives in adverb form.

1. **Typical** _____, an eyelash lives about 150 days.

2. At every moment your body is **busy** _____ replacing some of its 55 million cells.

3. **Unbelievable** _____, the air expelled by a sneeze travels 100 miles per hour.

4. **Usual** _____, your fingernails grow faster on the hand you use the most.

5. People are **basic** _____ healthiest between the ages of 5 and 15.

6. **Interesting** _____, a baby has 330 bones, while an adult has only 206.

Circle the correctly spelled adverb in each group.

1. tragicly   tragically   tragicily

2. sincerely   sincerly   sincerally

3. crazally   crazyly   crazily

4. annually   annualy   annualiy

17 SUFFIXES: *ful, less*

A *suffix* is a group of letters added at the end of a root word. When a suffix is added, the meaning of the root word changes. The suffix *less*, for example, means "without": A **homeless** person is without a home. The suffix *ful* means "full of": A **peaceful** person is full of peace.

A

What does each sentence describe? Add *ful* or *less* to the word that follows each sentence. Then write the new word on the writing line.

1. Michael tossed and turned in his bed all night.

   rest + _____ = _____

2. The howling noise from the swamp gave Matt goosebumps.

   fear + _____ = _____

3. Jenna locks all the doors and windows every evening.

   care + _____ = _____

4. Brad felt nothing when the dentist drilled his tooth.

   pain + _____ = _____

5. Wendy could hardly wait for her first parachute jump.

   fear + _____ = _____

6. Arnie feels sure that he will get the job he wants.

   hope + _____ = _____

7. The children didn't bother to lock their bicycles.

   care + _____ = _____

B

**To complete each sentence, add *ful* or *less* to a word from the box.
Hint: You will *not* use all the words.**

respect	hope	humor	tire	help
care	thought	worth	fear	power
pain	success	use	rest	spot

1. The human heart is a strong and _____ muscle.

2. The jeweler said that Jo's ring is a _____ fake.

3. The kitchen was _____ when Al finished cleaning.

4. All _____ students have learned good study skills.

5. Todd is polite and _____ to senior citizens.

6. Rita's _____ brother never laughs at her jokes.

C

**Puzzle answers are *synonyms* of the clue words. Create these synonyms
(words with the same meanings) by adding *ful* or *less* to words in the box.**

ACROSS

2. considerate
5. afraid
6. not hurting
7. useful
8. peaceful

DOWN

1. sloppy
2. endless energy
3. discouraged
4. not relaxed

31

There are no rules to help you with the suffixes *ise* and *ize*. Many more words end in *ize* than *ise*, however. But if you're not sure about a word, look it up in the dictionary!

A

Fill in the letter blanks with either *ise* or *ize*.

A French chef's recipe for Applesauce Surpr ___ ___ ___ cake once won a pr ___ ___ ___. The judges didn't real ___ ___ ___ that the "surprise" ingredient was chopped earthworms. To sanit ___ ___ ___ the worms, the chef had boiled them. Everyone recogn ___ ___ ___ d that the cake was delicious. But for some reason the chef was never able to popular ___ ___ ___ his recipe. Too many people seemed to desp ___ ___ ___ the idea of eating worms. Isn't it a shame that people are so quick to critic ___ ___ ___ a clever idea?

B

Write a word that ends in *ise* or *ize* to match each clue. Then use the new words to complete the crossword puzzle.

ACROSS

1. to make a summary

   _____

6. to run an ad

   _____

7. to list item by item

   _____

8. to make a revision

   _____

DOWN

2. to put energy into

   _____

3. goods that merchants sell

   _____

4. to give advice

   _____

5. to offer sympathy

   _____

SUFFIXES: *ant, ance, ancy, ent, ence, ency*

The suffixes *ant, ance, ancy, ent, ence,* and *ency* are added to many English root words. But watch out for spelling changes when the word ends in *e* or *t*.

EXAMPLE: serv~~e~~ + **ant** = serv**ant**   vacan~~t~~ + **cy** = vac**ancy**

A

Add *ance* or *ence* to the verbs in the box. Write each new word next to its definition.

perform	resist	tolerate	exist	persevere	prefer

1. _____ : willingness to live and let live

2. _____ : acting out; doing

3. _____ : withstanding opposition

4. _____ : liking one thing better than another

5. _____ : the condition of being

6. _____ : continued, patient effort

B

Add *ant* or *ent* to complete the words.

1. Ray is the superintend ___ ___ ___'s new assist ___ ___ ___.

2. How does an immigr ___ ___ ___ become a legal resid ___ ___ ___?

3. Mr. Hayes is a promin ___ ___ ___ merch ___ ___ ___ in town.

C

Circle two correctly spelled words to complete each sentence.

1. If you have a medical (emergency / emergancy) you should call an (ambulence / ambulance).

2. In (infancy / infency), children have a (tendancy / tendency) to get high fevers.

3. The principal was (insistant / insistent) that Harold have no more (absances / absences) from school.

4. Is a vitamin (deficiancy / deficiency) a (significant / significent) health factor?

20 — SUFFIXES: *ed, t, ing*

We use the suffixes *ed* and *t* to make the past tense form of a verb.
Notice that the *t* ending changes the spelling of the present tense verb.

EXAMPLES: walk, walk**ed**   bend, ben**t**

The suffix *ing* is used to show continuing action in the present.

EXAMPLES: walk**ing**   bend**ing**

To use these suffixes with verbs that end in *e* you must first
drop the final *e*

EXAMPLES: realiz~~e~~ + **ed** = realiz**ed**   realiz~~e~~ + **ing** = realiz**ing**

Add *ed* and *ing* to each of the verbs below.

	ed	ing
1. interrupt	_____	_____
2. possess	_____	_____
3. injure	_____	_____

You may add *ing* to a verb that ends in *y* without making any changes.
But before adding *ed*, you must change the *y* to *i*.

EXAMPLES: hurry + **ing** = hurry**ing**   hurr~~y~~ + **i** + **ed** = hurr**ied**

Circle the correctly spelled word in each group.

1. frying   friing   fryed   3. marrying   marryed   marriyd

2. buryed   burrying   buried   4. replyed   replied   repliing

Sometimes you must double the final consonant in a verb before adding
ed or *ing*. Usually, the consonant is doubled only after a *short* vowel.

EXAMPLES: bat + **t** + **ing** = bat**ting**   occur + **r** + **ed** = occur**red**

Add *ed* to the verbs on the left and *ing* to the verbs on the right.

1. copy _____   3. scurry _____

2. cry _____   4. delay _____

D

Complete the paragraph by circling the correctly spelled words.

No one is (considerred / considered) to be too (handicaped / handicapped) to compete in the Special Olympics. A boy with only one leg was once (awarded / awardded) a gold medal in gymnastics. It is a (stiring / stirring) sight to see these athletes (parading / paradeing) around the stadium before the games. Some of them are (making / makeing) their way on crutches or in wheelchairs. All the athletes have (spended / spent) months (prepareing / preparing) to compete. But none of them have been (worriying / worrying) too much about (loosing / loseing / losing). They know that while (wining / winning) is important, courage and determination are even *more* important. After (racing / raceing) to the finish line, every athlete who (competes / compettes) gets a ribbon and a hug.

E

Write the past tense form of each verb on the line. Then use these words to complete the puzzle.

ACROSS

1. stroke _____

4. imply _____

8. teach _____

9. apologize _____

10. determine _____

DOWN

2. try _____

3. spend _____

5. lose _____

6. drag _____

7. rip _____

21 — SUFFIX: *ous*

A noun takes the form of an adjective when the suffix *ous* is added. Nouns ending in *e* or *y* need special attention before this suffix is used.

With nouns ending in **e**, you will usually drop the **e** before adding *ous*. With nouns ending in **y**, you will first change the **y** to *i*.

EXAMPLES: nerve + **ous** = nerv**ous**   victory + **i** + **ous** = victor**ious**

A

Add the suffix *ous* to the following nouns.

1. mountain _____

2. melody _____

3. hazard _____

4. fame _____

5. danger _____

6. malice _____

B

Rewrite the boldfaced words to include the suffix *ous*.

RULE BREAKERS

A few nouns do *not* drop the final *e* before the suffix *ous* is added. Notice that these nouns end in *age*:

    courag**e**ous
    advantag**e**ous
    outrag**e**ous

And some nouns that end in *er* drop the *e*:

    monst**e**rous
    disast**e**rous

1. It was **grace** _____ of your friends to invite me for the weekend.

2. I love the **luxury** _____ accommodations.

3. The **monotony** _____ dripping of that faucet is quite annoying.

4. What a **marvel** _____ time we had on vacation this year!

5. The ship's **mystery** _____ disappearance has never been explained.

6. Some styles that were once fashionable now look **ridicule** _____ to us.

The suffixes *er* and *est* are used with adjectives to mean "more" and "most."

EXAMPLES: kind, kind**er**, kind**est**

If an adjective ends in **y**, change the **y** to *i* before adding *er* or *est*.

EXAMPLES: friendly, friendl**ier**, friendl**iest**

Complete the sentences with the correct form of the boldfaced word.

1. Standing as high as a two-story house, tyrannosaurus rex was **tall** _____ than most dinosaurs.

2. The **tall** _____, however, was brachiosaurus, whose head reached **high** _____ than a three-story building.

3. Compsognathus, the **tiny** _____ dinosaur, was about the size of a chicken.

4. At a length of 87 feet, diplodocus was the **long** _____ dinosaur of all.

5. The **hot** _____ temperature, 136.4 degrees, was recorded in Libya in 1922.

6. Measuring 3 feet across, the world's **large** _____ flower can be seen in Indonesia.

7. Even **strange** _____ than its mammoth size is the fact that this flower smells like rotting meat.

8. According to the *Guinness Book of World Records*, the world's **hard** _____ tongue twister is this:

    The sixth sick sheik's sixth sheep's sick.

A verb becomes a noun when the suffix *tion* or *sion* is added. The following rules will help you decide which suffix to use.

- Drop the final *e* if the root word ends in *se* or *te*; then add *ion*.
- Drop the final *e* if the root word ends in *ce*; then add *tion*.
- Add *ion* if the root word ends in *t*.
- If the root word ends in *d* or *de*, drop those letters and add *sion*.

Watch out for exceptions to these rules. Check a dictionary!

A

Fill in the letter blanks with *sion* or *tion*.

1. Opposums use imagina ___ ___ ___ ___ to outwit their enemies.

2. A glassy-eyed trance gives the impres ___ ___ ___ ___ that they're dead.

3. Did you know that bees dance as a form of communica ___ ___ ___ ___?

4. The preci ___ ___ ___ ___ of their dance shows other bees where to find food.

B

Use *tion* or *sion* to make a noun of each verb below. Then circle these words in the hidden word puzzle. Puzzle words may go up, down, backward, forward, or diagonally. Check off each word as you find it.

A	D	M	I	R	A	T	I	O	N	W	H
D	E	N	W	E	A	S	J	O	O	U	N
O	S	T	A	X	L	G	I	R	I	I	O
R	A	K	S	P	E	S	D	D	T	M	I
A	Y	M	O	R	N	T	E	H	A	P	T
T	W	H	A	E	E	C	T	W	E	R	A
I	L	B	T	S	I	V	E	W	R	E	N
O	M	E	A	S	G	N	I	T	C	S	I
N	R	S	I	I	N	H	V	S	E	S	M
P	N	O	L	O	Y	T	H	L	I	I	O
C	N	C	O	N	C	L	U	S	I	O	N
N	O	I	S	N	E	P	S	U	S	N	N
N	O	I	T	A	N	I	C	S	A	F	S

___ 1. admire _____

___ 2. express _____

___ 3. pretend _____

___ 4. nominate _____

___ 5. conclude _____

___ 6. adore _____

___ 7. revise _____

___ 8. suspend _____

___ 9. fascinate _____

___ 10. decide _____

___ 11. create _____

___ 12. impress _____

The word endings *ary* and *ery* can be very confusing. There are no rules to help you decide how to spell words with these suffixes. If you're not sure, use a dictionary.

A

Fill in the blanks with *ary* or *ery*. Then write the words on the lines.

1. Do you think unicorns are real or imagin ___ ___ ___?

   _____

2. How much station ___ ___ ___ will you need for those letters?

   _____

3. She gave her husband roses on their annivers ___ ___ ___.

   _____

4. Her younger sister is in element ___ ___ ___ school.

   _____

5. Slav ___ ___ ___ still exists in some parts of the world.

   _____

6. The stream marks the western bound ___ ___ ___ of her land.

   _____

B

Circle the correct spelling of each word. Then use the correctly spelled words to complete the puzzle.

ACROSS

1. sanitery
   sanitary
   saniterry

6. secretary
   secretery
   secratary

5. forgary
   forgarry
   forgery

7. cematary
   cemetary
   cemetery

DOWN

2. temperary
   temporary
   temperery

4. vocabulerry
   vocabulary
   vocabulery

3. nursery
   nersery
   nursary

25 **SUFFIXES**: *able, ible*

The word endings *able* and *ible* turn verbs and nouns into adjectives.

EXAMPLES: digest + **ible** = digest**ible**   accept + **able** = accept**able**

Before adding any suffix that begins with a vowel, you will usually drop the root word's final **e**.

pleasur~~e~~ + **able** = pleasur**able**

A

Circle the correctly spelled word in each pair of words.

1. responsible   responsable
2. irresistible   irresistable
3. disposeable   disposable
4. perishible   perishable

5. considerible   considerable
6. loveable   lovable
7. permissable   permissible
8. durible   durable

B

Complete each sentence by writing the correct form of the *boldfaced* word.

1. Is that price sticker easily **remove** _____ ?

2. Will the new gym be **access** _____ to wheelchairs?

3. Those **adore** _____ puppies will quickly find good homes.

4. Is your new raincoat **reverse** _____?

In some common words, the final *e* is **not** dropped before adding *able* or *ible*. Some of these rule-breakers are:

notic**e**able
chang**e**able
replac**e**able

5. If you have a bad driving record, you may not be **insure** _____.

6. It isn't **sense** _____ to stay out late on a school night.

Many words that name a person's job or special skill end in *or, er,* or *ian.*

EXAMPLES: invent**or**   teach**er**   magic**ian**

Read the clues. On each line, write the name of the job described. (The word will end with *or, er,* or *ian.*) Then find and circle that word in the hidden word puzzle. Puzzle words may go in any direction. Check off each word as you find it.

___ 1. one who repairs plumbing

_____

___ 2. one who solves technical problems

_____

___ 3. one who repairs electrical wiring

_____

___ 4. one who makes people laugh

_____

___ 5. one who mows the lawn

_____

___ 6. one who makes music

_____

___ 7. one who treats the sick

_____

___ 8. one who counsels about problems

_____

C	T	E	C	H	N	I	C	I	A	N
O	G	W	R	E	C	N	A	D	A	C
U	H	O	E	N	A	W	A	I	O	S
N	J	U	V	C	S	T	C	M	A	L
S	I	T	T	E	L	I	E	B	O	Y
E	A	O	G	A	R	D	E	N	E	R
L	R	K	S	T	I	N	D	Y	M	O
O	T	H	C	A	E	R	O	R	W	T
R	S	E	N	A	T	O	R	R	H	C
P	L	U	M	B	E	R	A	T	W	O
E	I	N	A	I	C	I	S	U	M	D

___ 9. one who dances

_____

___ 10. one who acts

_____

___ 11. one elected to the senate

_____

___ 12. one who governs a state

_____

27 — WORDS WITH *IE/EI*

The vowel combinations *ie* and *ei* cause many spelling problems. The rule of thumb on the right can often help you decide which spelling to use.

RULE OF THUMB
Use **i** before **e**
Except after **c**
Or when sounded like **a**
As in n**ei**ghbor or w**ei**gh.

i BEFORE *e*	*ei* AFTER *c*	*ei* WHEN SOUNDED LIKE *a*
sh**ie**ld	rec**ei**ve	sl**ei**gh
n**ie**ce	conc**ei**ted	**ei**ghteen

A

Fill in the blanks with *ie* or *ei*. Then write the completed word on the line.

_____ 1. Meg Green is my aunt, and I am her n_____ce.

_____ 2. Mike painted the c_____ling a light blue.

_____ 3. Al needs his rec_____pt to get a refund.

_____ 4. Mary is my next-door n_____ghbor.

_____ 5. Won't you have a p_____ce of this fresh apple pie?

_____ 6. You can't bel_____ve everything you hear.

_____ 7. Dark glasses sh_____ld your eyes from the sun.

_____ 8. Bill tried to dec_____ve us with that lie.

_____ 9. Sue works very hard to ach_____ve her goals.

B

Using the rule of thumb above to guide you, circle the correctly spelled word in each pair.

1. cheif / chief   5. eight / ieght

2. veil / viel   6. releif / relief

3. yield / yeild   7. grieve / greive

4. percieve / perceive   8. frieght / freight

A number of words with *ie/ei* are rule-breakers, however. You will have to look up their spellings in the dictionary until you memorize them!

EXAMPLES

l**ei**sure   effic**ie**nt

n**ei**ther   consc**ie**nce

s**ei**ze   suffic**ie**nt

 C

Circle the correctly spelled word in each sentence.

1. Which branch of (sceince / science) most interests you?

2. The pyramids of Egypt are (ancient / anceint) structures.

3. He bought that statue in a (foreign / foriegn) country.

4. (Wierd / Weird) sounds came from the haunted house.

5. It is a crime to make (counterfeit / counterfiet) money.

6. Did the miser name an (heir / hier) to his fortune?

 D

Read the clues. Then use words with the *ie* or *ei* spelling to complete the crossword puzzle.

ACROSS

3. eight plus ten

5. to find and bring back

6. frankfurter or hot dog

10. carriage for snow travel

DOWN

1. measure of distance from bottom to top

2. a loud, sharp cry

4. goods that are shipped

7. the daughter of a brother or sister

8. a king or queen's time on the throne

9. a bride's head covering

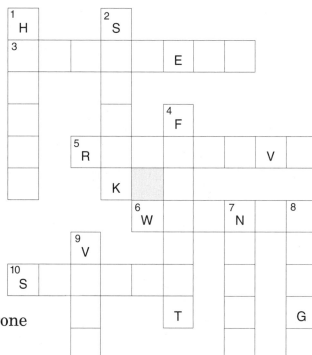

28 — REGULAR AND IRREGULAR PLURALS

The plural form of most singular nouns is easy to make. Simply add *s* to most words. Add *es* to words that end in **ch**, **s**, **sh**, **x**, or **z**.

EXAMPLES: star + **s** = star**s**   glass + **es** = glass**es**

book + **s** = book**s**   tax + **es** = tax**es**

A

Write the plural form of each word below.

1. fox _____   4. church _____

2. desk _____   5. candidate _____

3. dish _____   6. ghost _____

Some plural forms have their own special rules, however. Here's how to make plurals of words that end in *y*.

If the letter before the *y* is a vowel, add *s*:

valley + **s** = valley**s**   highway + **s** = highway**s**

If the letter before the *y* is a consonant, change the *y* to *i* and add *es*:

count + **ies** = count**ies**   berr + **ies** = berr**ies**

B

Circle the correctly spelled plural in each group.

1. librarys   libraryes   libraries

2. authorities   authoritys   authoritise

3. holidaies   holidays   holidayes

4. opportunitys   opportunities   opportunityes

For words that end with **f** or **fe**, first drop the **f** or **fe** and then add *ves*:

lea**f** + **ves** = lea**ves**   kni**fe** + **ves** = kni**ves**

Some exceptions to this rule are the plurals *beliefs, gulfs, roofs,* and *chiefs*. If you're not sure about a plural form, check your dictionary.

C

Write the correct plural form on each line.

1. one loaf, two _____ 3. one wife, four _____

2. one wolf, three _____ 4. one sheriff, five _____

Words that end in the long **o** sound can be tricky. Some plurals are made by adding *s* and some by adding *es*. To be certain, you must check the dictionary.

potato + **es** = potato**es** radio + **s** = radio**s**

D

**Circle the correctly spelled plural in each pair of words below.
Look up words you're unsure of.**

1. heros heroes 4. studioes studios

2. solos soloes 5. sopranos sopranoes

3. ratioes ratios 6. tomatos tomatoes

Irregular plurals do not follow any rules. But the chances are good that you have already memorized most of these common words.

E

Write a letter to match each singular noun on the left with its correctly spelled plural on the right.

1. ____ tooth
                      a. foots
                      b. childs
                      c. teeth

2. ____ child
                      d. oxen
                      e. children

3. ____ woman
                      f. womans
                      g. childern
                      h. feet

4. ____ foot
                      i. women
                      j. mouses

5. ____ mouse
                      k. mice

Many English words, like *butter* and *ladder*, have double consonants that make a single sound. So how can you decide whether to spell a word with one consonant or two? Listen to the *vowel* sound. Usually, double consonants appear after a *short* vowel.

EXAMPLES:	AFTER SHORT VOWELS	AFTER LONG VOWELS
	miss, not **mis**	**lazy**, not **lazzy**
	bell, not **bel**	**open**, not **oppen**

A

Study the examples above. Then underline the misspelled word in each sentence. Spell the word correctly on the line.

ASK YOURSELF:
Is the vowel sound long or short?

_____ 1. I recomend Paul for that job in the cafeteria.

_____ 2. Is it absolutely necesary to leave at 5 A.M.?

_____ 3. Larry's adress is 1422 Mountain View Avenue.

_____ 4. The shipwreck victims needed imediate help.

_____ 5. Sharon tries to take advantage of every oportunity.

_____ 6. Give me a chance and I won't disapoint you!

_____ 7. Carmen's new haircut gives her a diferent look.

_____ 8. Barry did an excelent job on his science project.

_____ 9. Selena's recent weight loss is quite aparent.

_____ 10. We were suposed to be home before dark.

B

Find a word in the box to complete each phrase.
Then fill in the missing letters.

across	apple	pretty	opportunity	terrible
possible	missile	paddle	collector	excellent
accident	ripple	address	embitter	correction

1. a stamp c __ __ __ __ __ __ __ r

2. a p __ __ __ __ y picture

3. a t __ __ __ __ __ __ e tornado

4. a __ __ __ __ s the street

5. a guided m __ __ __ __ __ e

6. an e __ __ __ __ __ __ __ t grade

7. your name and a __ __ __ __ __ s

8. a good business o __ __ __ __ __ __ __ __ __ y

C

Circle two correctly spelled words to complete each sentence.

1. Do you call the evening meal (super / supper) or (diner / dinner)?

2. His sister is a (professor / profesor) at a small (college / colege).

3. Should I use a (comma / coma) to (correct / corect) that sentence?

4. Will Sara (acept / accept) Sam's proposal of (marriage / mariagge)?

5. I made all the (arranggements / arrangements) for the
   (business / bussiness) meeting.

A Write a word that begins with *pre*, *pro*, or *per* to match each clue.

1. _____ : to look over in advance

2. _____ : to demonstrate against

3. _____ : to continue trying

B Use *er* and *est* to write forms of the adjective that compare.

1. **jolly** (MORE JOLLY) _____ (MOST JOLLY) _____

2. **sharp** (MORE SHARP) _____ (MOST SHARP) _____

3. **easy** (MORE EASY) _____ (MOST EASY) _____

C Read the prefix choices for each group of words. Complete each word by adding the correct prefix.

1. **un, im, il, in, ir** ___ ___ literate ___ ___ detected ___ ___ modest

   ___ ___ capable ___ ___ relevant ___ ___ available

2. **de, re** ___ ___ new ___ ___ claw ___ ___ mind

3. **dis, mis, sub** ___ ___ ___ station ___ ___ ___ regard

   ___ ___ ___ understand ___ ___ ___ miss

D Rewrite the words, adding the correct suffix.

1. **ly** possible _____ usual _____

   happy _____ frantic _____

2. **ed, t** spend _____ bury _____

   paint _____ sweep _____

3. **ing** speak _____ write _____ copy _____

4. **ous**   cavern_____   glory_____   suspicion_____

5. **ible, able**   adore _____   terror _____

6. **er, or, ian**   govern _____   play _____

magic _____   manage _____

7. **ful, less**   spot _____   beauty_____

E   Write the plural form of each noun.

wax _____   mess _____   woman _____

F   Circle the correctly spelled word in each pair.

swiming / swimming   ballad / balad   running / runing

G   Complete each word with the correct suffix.

1. **ence, ency ance, ancy**   coincid __ __ __ __   ambul __ __ __ __

emerg __ __ __ __   tru __ __ __ __

2. **ary, ery**   fish __ __ __   diction __ __ __

libr __ __ __   trick __ __ __

3. **ize, ise**   advert __ __ __   popular __ __ __

modern __ __ __   surpr __ __ __

4. **tion, sion**   expan __ __ __ __   reduc __ __ __ __

H   Complete each word with *ei* or *ie*.

rel __ __ f   dec __ __ ve   c __ __ ling   th __ __ f

IRREGULAR SPELLINGS

FOR HELP WITH THIS UNIT, SEE THE SPELLING REFERENCE GUIDE, RULES 26–43.

30 THE *AW* SOUND

The *aw* sound in English has different spellings in different words. Most often the *aw* sound is spelled **a, o, aw,** or **au**.

EXAMPLES:	— a —	— o —	— aw —	— au —
	c**a**ll	**o**ff	r**aw**	c**au**se
	w**a**ter	s**o**ng	h**aw**k	fr**au**d
	already	**o**fficer	l**aw**ful	**au**dience

Fill in the blanks with *a* or *o*. Write the words on the lines.

1. After his bath my d___g's coat feels very s___ft.

    _____   _____

2. Kirby ___ften w___lks instead of driving his car.

    _____   _____

3. Dana's ___ffice is just down the h___ll from mine.

    _____   _____

4. Lou saw that a l___g had f___llen across the path.

    _____   _____

5. How do you like your c___ffee, str___ng or weak?

    _____   _____

6. Does that recipe c___ll for peanuts or w___lnuts?

_____   _____

7. You ___lready added too much s___lt and pepper.

_____   _____

B

Read the clues. Then unscramble the words and write them on the lines. *Hint:* **All the words make the** *aw* **sound with either** *aw* **or** *au.*

1. the season after summer   **UMNUTA**   _____

2. something terrible   **FUWLA**   _____

3. something amazing   **WOSEEMA**   _____

4. a scarecrow's stuffing   **WARTS**   _____

C

Read the clues. Then complete the puzzle with words that make the *aw* **sound with either** *a* **or** *o.*

ACROSS

1. forever and ever

5. sweet flavoring made from cocoa beans

8. to speak

DOWN

2. not part, but the whole thing

3. ice crystals on a window or grass

4. used to write on a blackboard

6. quite frequently

7. throw

THE *AIR* SOUND

a **r**a**re** and **ve**ry
me**r**ry b**ear**

The *air* sound in English can be heard in the words *pair* and *wear*.
The usual spellings for this sound are **ar, er, air, are,** and **ear**.

EXAMPLES:

— ar —	— er —	— air —	— are —	— ear —
area	**ve**ry	h**air**	c**are**	p**ear**
libr**ar**y	**er**ror	ch**air**	sh**are**	t**ear**
app**ar**ent	station**er**y	d**air**y	bew**are**	b**ear**

A

**Read the words aloud. Circle the word in each group
that has the *air* sound.**

1. scary   spear   search
2. stain   stair   store
3. drain   dreary   dare

4. chance   chariot   clear
5. vanity   verdict   various
6. March   April   January

B

Rewrite the misspelled word in each sentence. *Hint:* **Listen for a
word that has the *air* sound.**

_____   1. That blonde girl's skin is very fare.

_____   2. Tod's rair coin is worth a lot of money.

_____   3. My mom's apple pie is beyond compear!

_____   4. You two boys will have to shere a book.

_____   5. Your father seems to be a devoted pearant.

_____   6. Ryan can help you repare your bicycle.

_____   7. Our class took the farryboat to Angel Island.

_____   8. It won't be necessery to wear a heavy coat.

_____   9. The climbers should bewair of the steep cliffs.

The *uh* sound in English is a troublemaker! Why?
Because *many* vowels can be pronounced this way.

EXAMPLES:

— a —	— e —	— i —	— o —
alive	oft**e**n	magn**i**fy	at**o**m
wom**a**n	ev**e**n	presid**e**nt	**o**ppose
breakf**a**st	happ**e**n	ind**i**vidual	pois**o**n

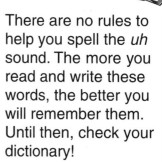

LOOK IT UP!

There are no rules to help you spell the *uh* sound. The more you read and write these words, the better you will remember them. Until then, check your dictionary!

 A

Say the words aloud. Then underline the vowel(s) in each word that has (have) the *uh* sound.

1. children   ago   canyon

2. banana   idea   several

3. again   item   riot

4. comma   agent   fortify

5. atom   fuel   arithmetic

6. weapon   senator   resident

 B

Find and circle the misspelled word in each sentence. Write the correctly spelled word on the line. Underline the vowel that says *uh*.

1. Did you finish the race in first or secund place? _____

2. I must write that appointment on my calandar. _____

3. Five students were absint from school today. _____

4. Ken bought a magezine at the supermarket. _____

5. Are you having any problems with your car? _____

6. Where did you purchise that wonderful hat? _____

7. How can I verafy the truth of your story? _____

8. Amy is in my third periud history class. _____

33 — THE *UHL* SOUND

Words that end with the *uhl* sound can be spelled in different ways. The three most common spellings are **le**, **al**, and **el**.

EXAMPLES:	— le —	— al —	— el —
	ab**le**	ov**al**	lev**el**
	need**le**	loy**al**	pan**el**

A

label

annual

squirrel

dual

gentle

quarrel

vital

handle

nickel

global

article

personal

people

ankle

natural

Complete the sentences with words from the box.

1. The company's _____ picnic is always held in June.

2. What I write in my diary is _____ and private.

3. It is _____ for rivers to flood in the spring.

4. The brain is one of the body's _____ organs.

5. When children _____ a lot, their parents become upset.

6. A _____ news report covers events around the world.

7. Will wrote his brother's address on the mailing _____.

8. Amy sprained her _____ playing basketball.

9. His _____ in the school paper was very interesting.

B

Circle the correctly spelled word in each set of parentheses.

1. Josie dusted the (mantel / mantal) over the fireplace.

2. Marty broke a (peddle / pedal / pedle) on his bike.

3. We like (maple / mapel) syrup on our pancakes.

4. Did you hear about the (fatal / fatle) traffic accident?

5. The baby has a (dimple / dimpel) in her cheek.

6. I had to (cancle / cancal / cancel) my weekend plans.

7. Were the ancient Greek gods (mortel / mortal) men?

8. Did you get a good grade on your (final / finle) test?

C

Underline the misspelled word in each sentence. Spell the word correctly on the line.

1. May I please have a nickle for my five pennies? _____

2. Lou saw a black squirral in that tall oak tree. _____

3. Are all those peopel in line for movie tickets? _____

4. The lable on the sweater says "Dry clean only." _____

5. Jason is very gentel with Daisy's new puppies. _____

6. My Halloween party has become an annule event. _____

7. Karen got a personel letter from the author. _____

8. Can you handal that problem all by yourself? _____

9. Hannah's new dancing shoes have ankel straps. _____

34 THE *UR* SOUND

chirp?
cherp?
churp?

The *ur* sound in English has a number of spellings. Usually the sound is spelled **ur, er, ir, or,** or **ar**.

EXAMPLES:

— ur —	— er —	— ir —	— or —	— ar —
b**ur**n	f**er**n	s**ir**	w**or**k	sug**ar**
t**ur**key	cl**er**k	g**ir**l	w**or**ship	coll**ar**
dist**ur**b	p**er**fect	th**ir**ty	att**or**ney	orch**ar**d

A

Quietly read each group of words aloud. Then cross out the word in each group that does *not* have the *ur* sound.

1. curb   bride   bird
2. cheer   chirp   were
3. altar   verse   wrist
4. germ   grid   worm
5. solar   brink   birth

6. reform   affirm   return
7. squirm   murder   near
8. crest   camera   molar
9. servant   silent   turmoil
10. calendar spur   spear

B

Find a word in the box that *rhymes* with each word listed below.
Write the rhyming word on the line.

shirt	collar	stir	herd	perfect
circle	nurse	regular	vinegar	thirsty
disturb	grammar	furniture	attorney	harbor

1. journey _____
2. dollar _____
3. hurt _____
4. verse _____
5. blur _____

6. hammer _____
7. third _____
8. barber _____
9. verb _____
10. miniature _____

56

C

Fill in the blanks with _er, ar,_ or _ir._ Then write the words on the lines.

1. Ed knows how to tie a p___fect slipknot. _____

2. My uncle owns a large h___d of cows. _____

3. She arranged the chairs in a big c___cle. _____

4. Don't put too much vineg___ in the salad dressing! _____

5. Do you know the rules of English gramm___? _____

6. Ten ships were anchored in the harb___. _____

D

Underline the misspelled word or words in each sentence.
Write the correctly spelled words on the lines.

1. The sign on her door said, "Do Not Disterb." _____

2. Manny was thursty after his long hike. _____

3. Mrs. Fenton is the nerse in my doctor's office. _____

4. The department store has a sale on oak firniture. _____

5. Your atturney will speak for you in court. _____

6. Carl is a regulor customer at my bookstore. _____

7. That pot of stew might birn if you forget to stur it.

   _____   _____

8. The coller on this old shurt is much too tight.

   _____   _____

35 — THE *oi* SOUND

The *oi* sound in English can be spelled in two ways: **oi** or **oy**. How can you decide which spelling to use?

- At the end of a word, the *oi* sound is most often spelled **oy**.

- When the *oi* sound comes before a vowel, it is also spelled **oy**.

- If the *oi* sound does not come at the end of a word or before a vowel, it is usually spelled **oi**.

EXAMPLES:

— oi —	— oy —
oil	t**oy**
c**oi**n	l**oy**al
v**oi**ce	empl**oy**

Fill in the blanks with *oi* or *oy*. Then write the words on the lines.

1. How many minutes does it take to b___l an egg? _____

2. Henry likes to put s___ sauce on his fried rice. _____

3. That new suntan lotion made my skin feel ___ly. _____

4. My aunt took a long v___age on a big cruise ship. _____

5. The cook put the sirl___n steak in the br___ler.

   _____   _____

6. The loud n___se in the machine shop ann___s everyone.

   _____   _____

7. She will be disapp___nted if she can't j___n the team.

   _____   _____

8. The r___al prince spent his b___hood in boarding school.

   _____   _____

9. Our empl___er called out to us in a loud v___ce.

   _____   _____

The *ow* sound in English is usually spelled **ow** or **ou**.

EXAMPLES:

— ow —	— ou —
c**ow**	**ou**t
g**ow**n	p**ou**nd
fl**ow**er	cl**ou**d

RULE OF THUMB

Where in a word does the *ow* sound most often appear?

• at the end of a word (all**ow**, ch**ow**)

• before *n* or *r* (**ou**nce, h**ou**r)

A

Find and circle two rhyming words in each list. *Hint:* **Listen for the *ow* sound.**

1. growl   foul   grown

2. pour   hour   sour

3. allow   yellow   somehow

4. powder   louder   launder

B

Read the clues. Use *ow* or *ou* to fill in the blanks.

1. to dig up a field   PL___ ___

2. what a ball does   B___ ___NCE

3. works at a circus   CL___ ___N

4. a woman's shirt   BL___ ___SE

C

Circle the misspelled word in each sentence. Spell the word correctly on the line.

1. King Arthur wore a golden croun.   _____

2. My uncle's howse is next door to yours.   _____

3. Do you know your vouels and consonants?   _____

4. I left my new touel by the swimming pool!   _____

5. The chef needs another pownd of sugar.   _____

6. Is the baby's hair blonde or broun?   _____

The *oo* spelling often has the *long u* sound as in *food* and *tool*. But in many words the *oo* spelling has a different sound. This is the sound you hear in words like *look* and *took*. This sound can also be spelled with the letters **u** or **ou**.

EXAMPLES:	— **oo** —	— **u** —	— **ou** —
	f**oo**t	p**u**t	c**ou**ld
	br**oo**k	f**u**ll	sh**ou**ld
	st**oo**d	b**u**sh	t**ou**r

A

Read each group of words aloud. Then cross out the word in each group that does *not* have the *oo* sound you hear in the word *foot*.

1. rookie   truly   fully

2. put   noon   hood

3. wood   fool   would

4. crook   cushion   crush

5. bully   balloon   overlook

6. bamboo   bushel   cookie

B

Fill in the blanks with *oo*, *u*, or *ou*.

1. Do you hear that b_____llfrog croaking?

2. Kim served chocolate p_____dding for dessert.

3. Max kicked the f_____tball over the goalposts.

4. Many t_____rists take pictures of the White House.

5. Joe planted a roseb_____sh by the front door.

6. This c_____kie dough needs more s_____gar!

7. He t_____k a handf_____l of coins from his pocket.

8. Why w_____ld she leave without saying g_____dbye?

9. Pete sh_____ld buy a noteb_____k before school starts.

The *ough* spelling appears in a number of common words. This spelling is very tricky because it can be pronounced in so many different ways. Unfortunately, there are no rules to help you decide when to use this letter combination.

A

Draw a line to match each word on the left with a rhyming word on the right.

Mough?

No, no! Moo!

1. rough   a. shoe

2. thorough   b. sew

3. through   c. taut

4. bough   d. burrow

5. dough   e. cow

6. bought   f. fluff

B

Write the correctly spelled word to complete each sentence.

1. In the 1500s, whooping (caugh / cough / colf) was treated by putting a live frog in the sick child's mouth. _____

2. The ancient Egyptians (thot / thawt / thought) that children could see into the future. _____

3. The first group that (sought / sawt / saught) help for abused children was the Society for the Prevention of Cruelty to Animals. _____

4. The shortest war ever (faught / fought / fawt) lasted only 38 minutes; England defeated Zanzibar. _____

5. (Although / Allthow / Allthough) money was scarce in the 1930s, you could buy a movie ticket for only 10 cents. _____

39 — WORDS WITH *AUGH, IGH*

The *augh* spelling makes the *aw* sound you hear in the word *awful*. The *igh* spelling makes the long *i* vowel sound you hear in the word *line*. In both spellings, the *gh* is silent.

A

Fill in the blanks with *augh* or *igh*.

In 845 A.D., the townspeople of Paris were filled with fr_____t. Some time during the n_____t, a longboat of Viking invaders had sailed up the river. The people knew they could not survive an onsl_____t by these fierce Norsemen. History books tell us that the French people were r_____t. Even though they put up a good f_____t, they were quickly c_____t and sl_____tered. The m_____ty Scandinavian raiders went on to terrorize Europe for the next 200 years.

B

Use the clues to complete the crossword puzzle.
Hint: All answers contain *augh* or *igh*.

ACROSS

2. flash of electricity in a stormy sky
4. a female offspring
6. badly behaved; mischievous
7. great joy and happiness
8. make a closer, firmer fit

DOWN

1. very strong and powerful
3. feeling of fear
5. instructed

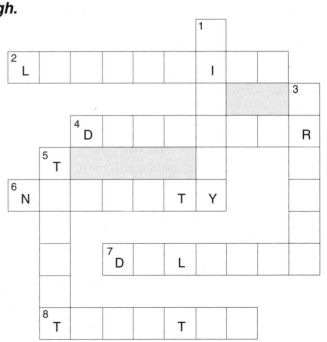

WORDS WITH *CEDE, CEED, SEDE*

40

The "seed" sound at the end of a word can be spelled in
different ways. The letter combinations *cede, ceed,* and
sede are the most common.

A

Use *cede, ceed,* or *sede* to complete the words in the paragraph.

     For Charles Darrow, bad luck pre_____d good luck in
1932. Having lost his job, Darrow pro_____ed to invent a
board game called *Monopoly*. He sold the first handmade sets
for $2.50 each. When he tried to sell *Monopoly* to a big game
company, the owners did not ac_____ to his wishes. Their
interest re_____d when they saw how long it took to play
a game. But Charles Darrow did not con_____ that their
opinion was correct. He was confident that *Monopoly* could
super_____ most other board games in popularity. So he
pro_____ed to make 5,000 more games and sell them to
local stores. Finally realizing that *Monopoly* would suc_____
in the marketplace, the big game company changed its mind and
bought the game. Ever since then, sales have ex_____ed
even Charles Darrow's wildest dreams.

B

Circle the correctly spelled word in each sentence.

1. In 1861, the 11 Confederate states decided to (succeed / sesed / secede)
   from the Union.

2. A man may get upset when his hairline begins to (recede / reseed).

3. Did the chicken (presede / precede) the egg, or did the egg come first?

63

The *kw* sound is spelled *qu* in almost all English words.

EXAMPLES: **qu**een s**qu**eeze fre**qu**ent

A

Circle the correctly spelled word in each group.

1. aquit   acquit   acquitt

2. squirrel   squirel   squerrel

3. quiz   quizz   quwiz

4. querk   quirk   quirrk

B

Find the misspelled word. Write it correctly on the line.

1. The quadruplets met for tea in a cquaint little cafe.

_____

2. The florist arranged the bowkay in a square vase.

_____

3. Do you know if Kwentin met his sales quota this month?

_____

4. Filling out this questionaire is really quite tiresome.

_____

C

Read the clues. Complete the puzzle with words containing *qu*.

ACROSS

2. looking wildly strange, unreal, twisted

4. formal dinner for many people

7. describes neglect of duty or harmful, unlawful behavior

8. of the same amount, size, or value

DOWN

1. story that begins where the first story ended

3. a characteristic of something's nature or character

5. enough; the necessary amount

6. still, peaceful; not noisy

WORDS WITH *CH, TCH* 42

In most words, the *ch* sound is spelled **ch** or **tch**.

The *ch* spelling appears at the beginning of a word, or just after a consonant or a long vowel sound.

The *tch* spelling is used after a short vowel sound.

EXAMPLES: **ch**impanzee   laun**ch**   pea**ch**

EXAMPLES: i**tch**ing   pa**tch**   wre**tch**ed

Circle the correctly spelled word in each pair.

1. tcheap   crunch   3. chuckle   bloch   5. ouch   cruch
2. birch   reatch   4. wich   pitchfork   6. latch   dich

Write a word containing *ch* or *tch* to match each clue.
Then find and circle the words in the hidden words puzzle.
Words may go up, down, across, backward, or diagonally.
Check off each word as you find it.

```
I  B  D  R  A  H  C  R  O  H
T  P  L  S  T  Y  B  I  O  C
C  I  F  E  T  C  H  P  E  A
H  T  H  B  A  K  S  N  S  N
A  C  T  H  S  C  H  C  A  I
T  H  W  R  O  E  H  F  H  P
C  E  O  T  H  A  R  T  C  S
H  R  C  F  M  C  P  I  R  R
E  H  S  P  T  O  T  D  U  Y
T  A  I  S  O  C  L  I  P  M
B  O  F  C  R  M  H  B  T  A
N  C  H  A  R  C  O  A  L  S
```

___ 1. small, short-handled ax
   *h*_____

___ 2. whitens laundry
   *b*_____

___ 3. briquets used to barbecue
   *c*_____

___ 4. stone tossing and hopping game
   *h*_____

___ 5. healthy green vegetable
   *s*_____

___ 6. commands a dog to return a ball
   *f*_____

___ 7. in-and-out of threaded needle
   *s*_____

___ 8. grove of fruit trees
   *o*_____

___ 9. the best; the titleholder
   *c*_____

___ 10. throws to the batter
   *p*_____

___ 11. to buy
   *p*_____

___ 12. slang word for *dog*
   *p*_____

65

WORDS WITH *J, G, GE, DGE*

The *j* sound you hear in the word *joy* can be spelled **j**, **g**, **ge**, or **dge**.

Before the vowels *a, o,* and *u*, spell this sound with a **j**.

EXAMPLES: **j**uice   **j**am   **j**og

At the end of a word, the *j* sound is almost always spelled **ge** or **dge**.

EXAMPLES: colle**ge**   fu**dge**   ba**dge**

A

Complete the words below with *j* or *g*.

1. en___oy

3. ban___o

5. ma___or

2. ___em

4. ra___e

6. ___iant

B

In each sentence, find two words in which the *j* sound is misspelled. Rewrite the sentences correctly.

1. Cabbaje is Gane's least favorite vegetable.

_____

2. Why did he go out gogging in his pagamas?

_____

3. That rickety old brige is danjerous.

_____

4. Are we all ready to recite the plege of allejiance?

_____

5. The jentlemen suddenly went on a rampadge.

_____

6. Do you have any knowlege of that difficult subgect?

_____

In some words, the *f* sound you hear may be spelled **ph**. These words can cause *mischieph* if you don't watch out *phor* them!

Find the spelling errors in each sentence. Rewrite the sentences correctly.

1. There are quite a phew phine pharmacies in Philadelphia.

   _____

2. My phriends Stephanie and Phrank are moving to Memfis, Tennessee.

   _____

3. A fysician must give you a fysical before you can play phootball.

   _____

4. I phelt *The Fantom of the Opera* was truly a fenomenal show.

   _____

B

Read the clues. Complete the puzzle with words containing the *ph* spelling.

ACROSS

1. indented section of a piece of writing

5. long piece of music for the full orchestra

6. A to Z sequence

8. study of Earth's features

DOWN

2. fake; not the real thing

3. part of a sentence

4. violent tropical cyclone

7. inscribed award; reminder of a victory or success

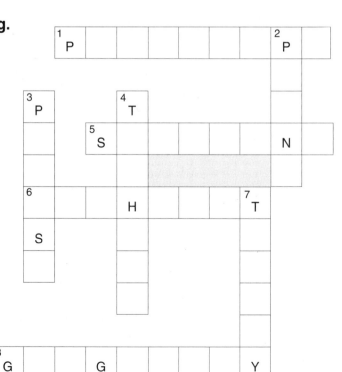

67

45 — SILENT LETTERS

Many words have letters that are not pronounced at all. It's easy to misspell these words by leaving out the silent letters.

A

In each word group, circle the word in which the given letter is silent.

1. **G** grinder   design   finger

2. **K** knapsack   kindred   ankle

3. **B** bumper   limber   plumber

4. **W** witness   wrist   wistful

5. **N** sonnet   solvent   solemn

6. **C** scene   crease   cease

7. **H** chore   coach   chrome

8. **E** plume   pelt   hem

9. **T** softer   after   often

10. **L** flap   half   alarm

B

Write sentences using the words you circled in Part A.

1. _____

_____

2. _____

_____

3. _____

_____

4. _____

_____

5. _____

_____

6. _____

_____

7. _____

_____

8. _____

_____

9. _____

_____

10. _____

_____

C

Fill in the blanks with silent letters.

1. According to fo___klore, creatures called ___nomes live under the earth.

2. Before we moved, I carefully ___rapped my collection of ___nick___nacks.

3. The chef has a special tec___nique for broiling s___ordfish.

4. No dou___t everyone enjoys the colors of the autum___ leaves.

5. The moonlight glis___ened on the snow and the ic___.

6. He needs s___issors and glu___ to finish his s___ience project.

D

Use the clues to solve the crossword puzzle. *Hint:* **All the answer words contain silent letters.**

ACROSS
1. yellow of an egg
3. powdered chocolate
6. to hurry
8. dance done on tiptoes
9. truthful

DOWN
1. small ship used for racing and pleasure cruises
2. shoelace tangle drawn tight
4. kitchen tool for slicing and carving
5. to go up the stairs
7. part of an act in a play; *Act 1, ___ 3*

69

— **C WITH THE SOUND OF S/K**

The *s* sound in a word can be spelled with either **c** or **s**. Likewise, the *k* sound can be spelled with either **c** or **k**.

EXAMPLES:	C WITH THE — SOUND OF S —	C WITH THE — SOUND OF K —
	ri**c**e	**c**rime
	nie**c**e	a**c**re

A

1. **Circle two words in which *s* makes the *s* sound.**

visible	Tuesday	resign	municipal
misery	whistle	sugar	vise

2. **Circle two words in which *c* makes the *s* sound.**

cousin	secretary	sauce	logical
cent	can't	traffic	category

3. **Circle two words in which *k* makes the *k* sound.**

knowledge	kitten	known	knitting
kettle	kneecap	knob	knight

4. **Circle two words in which *c* makes the *k* sound.**

sufficient	certain	column	receipt
perceive	vehicle	ceiling	farce

B

Notice the sound that *c* makes in each word below. Next to each word write another word in which *c* makes the same sound.

1. juice _____
2. curious _____
3. vacant _____
4. peace _____
5. anchor _____
6. space _____

C

Read the words in the box aloud. Find six words in which *c*'s are used to make *both* the *s* and the *k* sounds. Write the words on the lines.

counsel	cruise	access	concede	cocoa	practice
soccer	cancel	carcass	calcium	cactus	consequence

_____   _____

_____   _____

_____   _____

D

Notice that the boldfaced words in the clues are misspelled. (*Hint:* The *c*'s and *s*'s are mixed up.) Correct spellings of these words will complete the crossword puzzle.

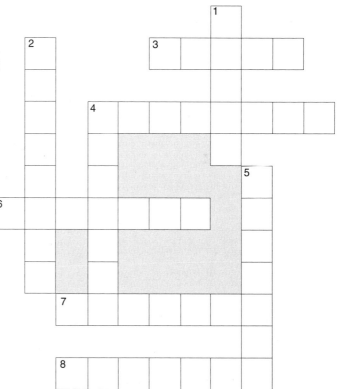

ACROSS

3. The general ordered the troops to **sease** firing.

4. That **desision** will be very hard to make.

6. If I pass the test, I will get my driver's **lisense**.

7. Are you absolutely **sertain** of your facts?

8. Were you **sinsere** in your offer to help?

DOWN

1. Decide whether each statement is true or **falce**.

2. It isn't easy to **sivilize** wild children.

4. Soldiers fight in **defence** of their country.

5. Can you explain your **absense** from class yesterday?

A Find two words in the box that contain each sound.
Write the words on the lines.

squirt	mobile	afraid	install	verify
flannel	arena	worship	marrow	clause

1. **AW** _____   _____

2. **AIR** _____   _____

3. **UH** _____   _____

4. **UHL** _____   _____

5. **UR** _____   _____

B Write a letter to match words that make the same sound
with a different spelling.

1. ____ boys   a. spite

2. ____ frowned   b. reseed

3. ____ tight   c. pound

4. ____ soot   d. noise

5. ____ recede   e. put

6. ____ nephew   f. missile

7. ____ worried   g. tribal

8. ____ bristle   h. curfew

9. ____ age   i. hurried

10. ____ bible   j. edge

C As you know, the *ough* letter combination makes different sounds in different
words. Write an example word containing *ough* for each sound listed below.

1. *uff* as in *stuff*: _____   3. *aw* as in *straw*: _____

2. *o* as in *go*: _____   4. *oo* as in *tool*: _____

D Find three misspelled words in each sentence. Correct the errors as you rewrite the sentences.

1. Boi Scouts try to be ahnest and trustwerthy.

   _____

2. Would you cair for a pare or a peatch?

   _____

3. I'd uppreciate it if you woodn't showt.

   _____

4. Phred ingured his gaw in the accident.

   _____

5. Indede, the juge must make a tuff decision.

   _____

6. The security gard enjoied the kwiet night.

   _____

7. Tcharles cut his nuckle on the broken bottel.

   _____

8. What is the cawse of the inkrease in tickit prices?

   _____

9. We wached the teatcher's demonstration vary closely.

   _____

10. His dawter frekwently overspends her buget.

    _____

SPELLING AND PUNCTUATION

FOR HELP WITH THIS UNIT, SEE THE SPELLING REFERENCE GUIDE, RULES 44–46.

UNIT
4

47 — THE APOSTROPHE

The *apostrophe* (') is used to show ownership or possession. When the apostrophe is omitted or misplaced, a word is considered misspelled.

EXAMPLES:

WITH SINGULAR NOUNS: **Nicole's   town's   giraffe's**

WITH PLURAL NOUNS NOT ENDING IN *S*: **people's   women's**

WITH PLURAL NOUNS ENDING IN *S*: **boys'   states'   countries'**

A

Rewrite the nouns to show possession.

1. a fishs gills

_____

2. childrens toys

_____

3. a chickens coop

_____

4. Shakespeares sonnets

_____

5. cities mayors

_____

6. mices nest

_____

Home Sweet Home

The apostrophe is also used to show the plurals of letters, numbers, symbols, abbreviations, and words used as illustrations.

EXAMPLES: Her **T's** look just like **7's**.

Are there two **k's** in bookkeeper?

All the **M.D.'s** are in a meeting.

He uses too many **!'s** in his writing.

Her speech is full of **and's** and **but's**.

B

Study the five examples at the bottom of page 74. Now write an example sentence of your own to show correct placement of the apostrophe.

1. (PLURAL LETTERS) _____

   _____

2. (PLURAL NUMBERS) _____

   _____

3. (PLURAL SYMBOLS) _____

   _____

4. (PLURAL ABBREVIATIONS) _____

   _____

5. (PLURAL WORDS AS ILLUSTRATIONS) _____

   _____

Use an apostrophe to show where a letter or number has been omitted.

EXAMPLES: IN CONTRACTIONS: **won't   shouldn't   they're**
            IN DATES: **the class of '99   Superbowl '86**

C

Rewrite the phrase or sentence correctly.

1. Im leaving now.

   _____

2. the "96" Oscars

   _____

3. Wear you're gloves.

   _____

4. Youl'l need a coat.

   _____

5. the blizzard of 88'

   _____

6. He coul'dve helped.

   _____

7. Its time to study.

   _____

8. Theyd' better hurry.

   _____

An *abbreviation* is a short way to write a word or a phrase. Using abbreviations saves time, space, and energy.

EXAMPLES: Ms. Kelly   Y.M.C.A. or YMCA
              A.M.   Sen. Hector J. Hawthorne
              U.S. or US   Beatrice French, M.D.

⬡A

Social titles and titles of rank are usually abbreviated. Write a letter to match each abbreviation on the left with a complete word on the right.

1. _____ **Mr.**		a. Colonel
2. _____ **Dr.**		b. Senator
3. _____ **Jr.**		c. Sergeant
4. _____ **Rev.**		d. Lieutenant
5. _____ **Gov.**		e. Junior
6. _____ **Sen.**		f. Mister
7. _____ **Sgt.**		g. Reverend
8. _____ **Lt.**		h. Governor
9. _____ **Gen.**		i. Doctor
10. _____ **Col.**		j. General

⬡B

On the line below each phrase, write the complete word or words represented by the abbreviation.

1. twelve **oz.** of gold

   _____

2. a bill marked **pd.**

   _____

3. deliver a **pkg.**

   _____

4. located in **bldg.** B

   _____

5. **asst.** to the president

   _____

6. priced at 25¢ **ea.**

   _____

C

Circle the correctly spelled abbreviations. After each sentence, write the complete words on the lines.

1. How many (qts. / quas. / qrts.) are in a (gall. / gal. / gln.)?

   _____   _____

2. What is your (heght. / ht. / heit.) and (wt. / wgt. / weigh.)?

   _____   _____

3. Do you live on State (Str. / St.) or Grand (Boul. / Blvd.)?

   _____   _____

4. How many (fets. / ft. / fts.) are in 6 (yrds. / y.d. / yds.)?

   _____   _____

5. Are there 720 (mn. / mnt. / mins.) in 12 (hrs. / hor. / H.R.)?

   _____   _____

6. How many (yr. / yrs.) of (expe. / exp.) do you have?

   _____   _____

D

Write the abbreviation next to each word. If you need help, check a dictionary!

1. miles per hour _____   7. number _____

2. Before Christ _____   8. etcetera _____

3. Avenue _____   9. chapter _____

4. month _____   10. corporation _____

5. plural _____   11. anonymous _____

6. government _____   12. Bachelor of Science _____

77

A *hyphen* (-) is used to join or separate words in certain circumstances. Words in which necessary hyphens are missing or misplaced are considered misspelled.

In writing out numbers, hyphens are used in two situations.

1. Hyphens join compound numbers from twenty-one to ninety-nine.

   EXAMPLES: twenty-seven   forty-nine   eighty-three

2. Hyphens punctuate fractions used as adjectives.

   EXAMPLES: two-thirds majority   a **one-half** interest

⟨A⟩

Write *C* if the number is spelled and punctuated correctly. If the hyphen is missing or misplaced, rewrite the number.

1. nine-teen _____

2. seventy five _____

3. sixtytwo _____

4. fifty-five _____

5. thirty-6 _____

6. one-hundred-ten _____

A hyphen is always used in words with the prefixes *self, ex,* and *all.*

EXAMPLES: self-confident   ex-athlete   all-encompassing

A hyphen is used with all prefixes before a proper noun, a proper adjective, or the name of an office.

EXAMPLES: mid-March   pro-American   ex-president

⟨B⟩

Write *C* if the spelling and punctuation are correct. Rewrite the word or words if you see an error.

1. former mayor _____

2. anti-French _____

3. post WWII _____

4. All American _____

5. ex ambassador _____

6. sub-Saharan _____

A hyphen is used to connect some compound nouns.

EXAMPLES: cure-all   great-grandmother

C

Write _C_ if the word is correct. Rewrite the word if there is an error in spelling or punctuation.

LOOK IT UP!

The use of hyphens in compound words often changes over time. The hyphens tend to disappear as words become more familiar. It is always best to check an up-to-date dictionary!

1. hand-bag

_____

2. forget-me-not

_____

3. bull's eye

_____

4. horse-shoe

_____

5. father in law

_____

6. Indo-European

_____

7. ill timed

_____

8. court-martial

_____

9. African American

_____

10. north-east

_____

11. delegate at large

_____

12. halftruth

_____

13. lead-in

_____

50 — USING A DICTIONARY

Read the dictionary entry words in the chart. Study the punctuation used.

dou•ble-head•er	mpg	self-as•sured
Mme.	blue•bird	pow•er plant
mid•day	ex-judge	all-out
re•type	esp.	made-to-or•der

A

Write *T* or *F* to show whether each statement about dictionary entry words is *true* or *false*.

1. _____ The punctuation of an entry word shows how the word is pronounced.

2. _____ Dots are used to divide an entry word into syllables.

3. _____ Hyphens used in an entry word are part of that word's spelling.

4. _____ When listed as entry words, all abbreviations end in a period.

5. _____ A space is used to divide all two-part nouns that appear as one entry word.

6. _____ Abbreviations of social titles are never listed as entry words.

B

Use the information in the chart of entry words to answer the questions.

1. How many syllables are in the noun *power plant*? _____

2. What listing is the abbreviation of *Madame*? _____

3. What compound noun is hyphenated? _____

4. What listing is the abbreviation of *especially*? _____

80

Apostrophes and hyphens have been omitted or misused in the following sentences. Find two errors in each sentence. Rewrite the sentences correctly on the writing lines.

1. Theres a huge, two story building on Ellis Island.

_____

2. The building face's the sky-line of New York City.

_____

3. From 1892 until the mid 1920's some 16-million immigrants entered this great hall.

_____

_____

4. Theyd all arrived there in they're ships' steerage sections.

_____

_____

5. In 1903, a passengers' ticket from Europe to the United States cost about thirty four dollars.

_____

_____

6. When you visit, you'l enjoy Ellis Islands' many displays.

_____

B Abbreviate the boldfaced words.

1. **District** of **Columbia** _____   5. **capital** letter _____

2. **United States of America** _____   6. **lowercase** letter _____

3. **ante meridiem** (morning) _____   7. 90° **Fahrenheit** _____

4. **post meridiem** (afternoon) _____   8. **Bachelor of Science** _____

C Circle the compound words that are correctly spelled and hyphenated.

stepfather   moth-eaten   thirty one   exjudge

nest egg   anteater   pro-Castro   self esteem

grand-son   father-in-law   antifreeze   great aunt

D Study the dictionary entry words. Then answer the questions.

feath•er bed	**tomb•stone**	**ci•ty-state**
sin•gle-hand•ed	**hush pup•py**	**in•ter•per•son•al**

1. Which entry word is a two-syllable compound noun without a hyphen?

_____

2. Which entry word has five syllables?

_____

3. Which hyphenated compound noun has three syllables?

_____

4. In which entry word is a hyphen used to connect two parts of an adjective?

_____

5. Which two nouns are made up of two unconnected words?

_____

DAYS OF THE WEEK — 51

Sunday (Sun.)
Monday (Mon.)   **Thursday (Thurs.)**
Tuesday (Tues.)   **Friday (Fri.)**
Wednesday (Wed.)   **Saturday (Sat.)**

A

Read the names of the days aloud. Listen to the sounds. Then answer the questions.

SUN.	MON.	TUES.	WED.	THURS.	FRI.	SAT.
	1	2	3	4	5	6

1. Which day has three syllables?

   _____

2. Which day has the long *u* sound as in *grew*?

   _____

3. Which two days have silent letters?

   _____

   _____

4. Which day has the long *i* sound as in *spy*?

   _____

5. Which three days have the *z* sound as in *was*?

   _____

   _____

   _____

B

Do you know which day of the week you were born? This anonymous old nursery rhyme begins with the first day of the workweek. Fill in the blanks.

_____'s child is fair of face,

_____'s child is full of grace,

_____'s child is full of woe,

_____'s child has far to go,

_____'s child is loving and giving,

_____'s child works hard for a living,

But a child that's born on the Sabbath day
Is fair and wise and good and gay.

MONTHS OF THE YEAR

January	April	July	October
February	May	August	November
March	June	September	December

A

Read the names of the months aloud. Listen to the sounds. Then answer the questions.

1. Which three months rhyme with the word *remember*?

   _____

   _____

   _____

2. Which two names rhyme with the word *strawberry*?

   _____

   _____

3. Which three months have just one syllable?

   _____

   _____

   _____

4. The first letter of which month says the letter's *name* as well as the sound of the letter?

   _____

   _____

B

To save time and space, the names of the days and months are often abbreviated. Circle the correct abbreviations.

1. **January** Jny. Janu. Jan.
2. **February** Feb. Febr. Feby.
3. **March** Mch. Mar. Mach.
4. **April** Apr. Apl. Ap.
5. **May** My. not abbreviated
6. **June** Jne. Jun. J.
7. **July** Jly. Jul. Jne.
8. **August** Aug. Ag. Augu.
9. **September** Sep. Sept. Spt.
10. **October** Oc. Oct. Octo.
11. **November** Nov. Nv. Nvr.
12. **December** Dcbr. Dece. Dec.

C

Write complete words for these abbreviated dates.

1. Sat., Aug. 18 _____

2. Thurs., Jul. 4 _____

3. Tues., Mar. 29 _____

NUMBERS AS WORDS 53

The following rules can help you decide when to use spelled-out numbers in your written work.

1. Spell out numbers of one hundred or less.
   (six, seventy)

2. Spell out numbers that are rounded to hundreds and that can be written in two words or less.
   (one thousand, five hundred)

3. Spell out any number that begins a sentence (or rewrite the sentence). **(Sixteen ships sailed.)**

4. Spell out ordinal numbers. **(first, tenth)**

5. Spell out an expression of time unless it is a *specific* time using A.M. or P.M. **(four o'clock, 4 P.M.)**

─── DON'T FORGET! ───

You've already learned that hyphens are used in the spelling of fractions used as adjectives and in compound numbers from twenty-one through ninety-nine.

two-thirds pay
seventy-six

A

Circle the correct spelling of each number.

1. bilyun   billion
2. million   milion
3. fourty   forty

4. thowsand   thousand
5. thirty two   thirty-two
6. hunderd   hundred

7. ninety   ninty
8. elevin   eleven
9. eight   eaght

B

Use the *th* suffix to spell out the adjective form of each numeral.

EXAMPLES: 5, fifth   10, tenth

1. **12,** _____
2. **20,** _____
3. **8,** _____

4. **100,** _____
5. **14,** _____
6. **97,** _____

C

Rewrite to correct the errors.

1. 6 o'clock _____
2. fourty two _____
3. ten A.M. _____

4. one fourth cup _____
5. seconth _____
6. 5 flags flew. _____

54 — STATE NAMES AND ABBREVIATIONS

Write the full name of each state after its official postal abbreviation. Some abbreviations, such as *NY* and *FL*, are easy to figure out. Others, like *MI, MO, MS, MA, MT,* and *ME* may take some concentration to get straight. *Hint: The number of letters in each state's name appears in parentheses.*

1. **AL** _____ (7)

2. **AK** _____ (6)

3. **AZ** _____ (7)

4. **AR** _____ (8)

5. **CA** _____ (10)

6. **CO** _____ (8)

7. **CT** _____ (11)

8. **DE** _____ (8)

9. **FL** _____ (7)

10. **GA** _____ (7)

11. **HI** _____ (6)

12. **ID** _____ (5)

13. **IL** _____ (9)

14. **IN** _____ (7)

15. **IA** _____ (4)

16. **KS** _____ (6)

17. **KY** _____ (8)

18. **LA** _____ (9)

19. **ME** _____ (5)

20. **MD** _____ (8)

21. **MA** _____ (13)

22. **MI** _____ (8)

23. **MN** _____ (9)

24. **MS** _____ (11)

HAVE YOU NOTICED?

Postal abbreviations do not include periods.

25. **MO** _____ (8)   38. **PA** _____ (12)

26. **MT** _____ (7)   39. **RI** _____ (5, 6)

27. **NE** _____ (8)   40. **SC** _____ (5, 8)

28. **NV** _____ (6)   41. **SD** _____ (5, 6)

29. **NH** _____ (3, 9)   42. **TN** _____ (9)

30. **NJ** _____ (3, 6)   43. **TX** _____ (5)

31. **NM** _____ (3, 6)   44. **UT** _____ (4)

32. **NY** _____ (3, 4)   45. **VT** _____ (7)

33. **NC** _____ (5, 8)   46. **VA** _____ (8)

34. **ND** _____ (5, 6)   47. **WA** _____ (10)

35. **OH** _____ (4)   48. **WV** _____ (4, 8)

36. **OK** _____ (8)   49. **WI** _____ (9)

37. **OR** _____ (6)   50. **WY** _____ (7)

55 — MEASUREMENT TERMS

People use measurement to understand things, to make things, and to purchase things. Knowing how to spell and abbreviate measurement terms can help you at home, at school, in the marketplace, or on the job.

No doubt you are already familiar with many Standard U.S. units of measurement. Study the words in the chart.

LENGTH:	inch	foot	yard	furlong	mile
AREA:	acre	square mile			
LIQUID CAPACITY:	ounce	pint	quart	gallon	barrel
DRY CAPACITY:	pint	quart	peck	bushel	
WEIGHT:	dram	ounce	pound	ton	

A

Write a letter to match each term with its abbreviation. Then draw a line to match each abbreviation with the kind of thing it measures.

1. _____ **inch**   a. pt.   wheat

2. _____ **pound**   b. bu.   ice cream

3. _____ **square mile** c. in.   a wildlife refuge

4. _____ **bushel**   d. sq. mi.   a playing card

5. _____ **pint**   e. lb.   bag of sugar

B

Write a term from the chart to complete each sentence.

1. A _____ of peaches is equal to 8 quarts.

2. A _____ is 5,280 feet in length.

3. A _____ is a weight of 2,000 pounds.

4. A _____ is 36 inches long.

C

Write the complete term represented by the abbreviation.

1. 5,000 bb. of oil

   _____

2. 1 oz. of fine perfume

   _____

3. a qt. of strawberries

   _____

4. 2 ft. of rope

   _____

5. a 6-fur. horserace

   _____

6. a trip of 500 mi.

   _____

7. 10 gal. of gasoline

   _____

8. a flood covering 3 sq. mi.

   _____

The *Metric System* of measurement is becoming more common in the United States. Study the information about metric measurement in the chart.

LENGTH:	**meter**	(3.3 feet)	abbreviation: **m**
WEIGHT:	**gram**	(.035 ounces)	abbreviation: **g**
CAPACITY:	**liter**	(1.06 quarts)	abbreviation: **l**

The following prefixes are used with these basic units to indicate exact amounts.

milli	(one-thousandth)	**deca**	(times 10)
centi	(one-hundredth)	**hecto**	(times 100)
deci	(one-tenth)	**kilo**	(times 1,000)

D

Circle the word that correctly completes each sentence.

1. Your sides might burst if you drank a (decaliter / deciliter) of soda pop.

2. Distance between towns could be measured in (millimeters / kilometers).

3. The door to your house is about 1 (m / l) wide.

4. A big bag of potatoes could be weighed in (kilograms / decigrams).

5. A small pile of gold dust might weigh 4 (m / g).

6. Your little fingernail is about 1 (centimeter / centigram) wide.

A Write the correctly spelled and abbreviated form of each date.

1. Monday, January 30

_____

2. Tuesday, February 2

_____

3. Wednesday, March 21

_____

4. Thursday, April 1

_____

5. Friday, May 15

_____

6. Saturday, June 7

_____

7. Sunday, July 27

_____

8. Tuesday, August 9

_____

B Write the complete name of each month next to its abbreviation.

1. Sept. _____

2. Oct. _____

3. Nov. _____

4. Dec. _____

C Write the correct U.S. postal abbreviation next to each state.

ME	MD	MA	MI	MN	MS	MO

1. Missouri _____

2. Maine _____

3. Mississippi _____

4. Maryland _____

5. Minnesota _____

6. Massachusetts _____

7. Michigan _____

D Read the names of the state capitals and the state postal abbreviation. Write the complete name of each state.

1. Lincoln, NE

_____

2. Springfield, IL

_____

3. Juneau, AK

_____

4. Dover, DE

_____

5. Des Moines, IA

_____

6. Atlanta, GA

_____

7. Topeka, KS

_____

8. Hartford, CT

_____

E Complete the sentences with abbreviations from the box.
Hint: You will *not* use all the abbreviations.

sq. mi.	lbs.	ft.	in.	km	ml

1. A newborn baby is usually about 20 _____ in length.

2. There are only 1,212 _____ in Rhode Island, our smallest state.

3. Mount McKinley in Alaska rises 20,320 _____ above sea level.

4. Each fall, the Arctic tern flies 18,000 _____ to Antarctica.

F Spell out the following numbers. Use correct punctuation.

1. **47** _____

2. **2/3** _____

3. **621** _____

4. **95** _____

5. **1,000** _____

6. **3rd** _____

56 — *A, B, C* WORDS

A

Circle 11 correctly spelled words to complete the paragraph. Then write the words on the lines.

Every (awtum / autumn), twenty rock stars put on a (benefit / benifit) performance for crippled children. (Committee / Comitee) members are (bizily / busily) planning the event (allready / already). The (auditorium / audittorium) they select must be (convenently / conveniently) located, (accesible / accessible) to wheelchairs, and large enough to (accomodate / accommodate) a huge crowd. Since all proceeds go to (charity / chairity), no one minds that there are no tickets at (bargin / bargain) prices.

1. _____
2. _____
3. _____
4. _____
5. _____
6. _____
7. _____
8. _____
9. _____
10. _____
11. _____

B

Rewrite each clue word correctly. Complete the puzzle with the correctly spelled words.

ACROSS

2. canidate _____

5. accuse _____

6. accross _____

DOWN

1. catugory _____

3. accurracy _____

4. amachur _____

A

Circle correctly spelled words to complete the sentences.

1. Are you (disatisfied / dissatisfied), or
   perhaps even (desparate / desperate),
   about the (effectiveness / affectiveness)
   of your (deodorant / deodarant)?

Hurry! Get your *Stink-Stop* before it's all gone!

2. I want to (familiarize / fam015arize) you
   with an (extrordinary / extraordinary)
   new product that will (fulfill / fullfill)
   your needs (exstreemly / extremely) well.

3. I do not (exaggerate / exxagerate) when I declare
   that your (disappointment / dissappointment) and
   (embarassment / embarrassment) will be gone for good.

4. If *Stink-Stop* does not make a (defanite / definite)
   improvement in your social (environment / envirement),
   I will gladly (forfit / forfeit) the purchase price.

5. Since there is no (financial / financhul) risk to you, what
   (exccuse / excuse) could you have (four / for) turning down
   this very (fare / fair) offer?

B

Find the spelling errors. Rewrite the corrected word.

1. Are you driveing or am I?

2. This lemon pie is delicous.

3. Is that the emporer's palace?

4. Fine china is very fragil.

A

Underline 15 spelling errors. Then rewrite the paragraph correctly.

I gess you havn't herd the news. We half an incredable new
animal at the zoo! Its a young mail guerilla named Koko. When
he is fully groan, he will way 400 pounds and reach a hieght of
about six feet. You should go to sea hymn imediately. He's grate!

_____

_____

_____

_____

_____

B

**Spell the words correctly on the
writing lines. Then find and circle
each word in the hidden words
puzzle. Words may go up, down,
across, backward, or diagonally.
Check off each word as you find it.**

```
N O H O N O R A B L E W L I
T E H H T I F E O R L A G O
I E M E A N S T E O T C O T
N T H E A R I T D I E G O S
S N F T A H A E P R O C U E
U A N O T U R S Y E H T E R
R R H Q D I O C S K B R O E
A A W A F H X J U M O V E T
B U R T E H L Z A Y E B R N
L G U A R D T N A R O N G I
E O H H I N T E R P R E T E
```

1. ___ gaurd _____

2. ___ hoarce _____

3. ___ gos _____

4. ___ ignerant _____

5. ___ hospitle _____

6. ___ interpet _____

7. ___ insureable _____

8. ___ honerable _____

9. ___ intrest _____

10. ___ gradguate _____

11. ___ garantee _____

12. ___ harrassment _____

A

Underline 17 spelling errors. Then rewrite the paragraph correctly.

My loiyer warned me knot to lone any of my luckshurious belongings to strangers. But I was lonly and trying to be likeable. I also had no nowlidge of how jelous some people can be. Loosing my jewulry was bad enough, but I really knead my limozine. If I new then what I no now, I would have at leased lissened to my loyer!

_____

_____

_____

_____

_____

_____

_____

B

Circle the *correctly* spelled words.

1. It is the (juge's / judge's) job to see that (justice / justise) is done.

2. The scientist (led / lead) me into his (labratory / laboratory) to show me his latest experiment.

3. All of our (knifes / knives) are kept in the (kitchen / kichen).

4. Today, our (literatur / literachur / literature) (lesson / lessen) included a (lovely / lovly) story.

A

Rewrite the misspelled words. Then write an original sentence using each pair of words.

1. **ninty nickles** _____ _____

   _____

2. **outragous occurence** _____ _____

   _____

3. **minature marshmellows** _____ _____

   _____

4. **neccesary nutrision** _____ _____

   _____

5. **ordnary orkestra** _____ _____

   _____

B

Rewrite each clue word correctly. Complete the puzzle
with the correctly spelled words.

ACROSS

1. originel _____

5. neice _____

6. mathmatics _____

7. newsance _____

DOWN

1. wunce _____

2. nuculus _____

3. obstucle _____

4. ommision _____

A

Complete the paragraph by circling the correctly spelled words.

Is the (persistant / persistent) (rumer / rumor) true? Or has there been a (rescent / recent) change in our (personal / personnel) department's hiring (practices / practises)? (Problems / Problams) have become (prevelent / prevalent) since Bert and Gert came to work here. Who could (possably / possibly) have (reccomended / recommended) them? No one would have given such (unqualified / unqualafied) people a good (reference / referrence). How could they have (passed / past) the entry-level test? And I'm (quiet / quite) (preturbed / perturbed) about their chumminess with management. Doesn't it seem (paculiar / peculiar) that they call the boss "Dad"?

B

Find the spelling errors. Rewrite the sentences correctly.

1. Penny pozeses the right phiscal qualitys to enter the beauty pagent.

_____

_____

2. Prominant politisians probaly expect to be put on a pedestel.

_____

_____

3. Ray didn't relize the rehersal would involve so much repitition.

_____

_____

A

Underline 33 spelling errors. Then rewrite the paragraph correctly.

Tune in toknight too *Terrer on Tusday*. Undoutedly, this new sieries is something speshul—knot your ushual teevee fair! First thyme ever shone on telavision. The suspence in these previously untolled tails may tern your stomack. Some seens are sew scarey it's unbelivible! Warning: Sevral storeys are to shoking for the unsofisticated. Sea tonite's skedjool for details. Tommorrow will be two late!

_____

_____

_____

_____

_____

_____

B

Spell the words correctly on the writing lines. Then find and circle each word in the hidden words puzzle. Words may go up, down, across, backward, or diagonally. Check off each word as you find it.

```
S I M A E G I S H A K Y N U
U E T H R U E S N N T H N N
S A R T R E Q D O O E T Y M
A U V G E N W I L H I E L I
B Y P O E W T E N L I T T S
L M D E R A R E A H R M C T
E I N O R A N G F A C A I A
W H I A N V T T G E C E R K
H R P C I S I E T M A S T A
J E E U S T D S L K I E S B
S T E H O Y N E O S U S E L
U N N A T U R A L R T K N E
```

1. ___ unatural _____

2. ___ supervizer _____

3. ___ tradgedy _____

4. ___ techneek _____

5. ___ useable _____

6. ___ strickly _____

7. ___ tolerence _____

8. ___ shakey _____

9. ___ sargent _____

10. ___ untill _____

11. ___ seperation _____

12. ___ unmistakeable _____

Underline three misspelled words in each sentence.
Rewrite the sentences correctly.

1. Your probably aware that Lex Luthor and Brainiac are the villans who try to rest power from Superman.

   _____

   _____

2. Because residents there are listed by *first* names, visiters to Iceland waist valueable time looking up phone numbers.

   _____

   _____

3. During a violant thunderstorm, litening may strike a vary tall building several times.

   _____

   _____

4. Wood you believe that each man who sailed with Columbus drank two-thirds of a gallan of whine per day?

   _____

   _____

5. Blue wails way more than any other creature in the werld.

   _____

   _____

6. When volcanos erupt, the surrounding vegitation vannishes under hot lava.

   _____

   _____

A Circle the word that correctly completes each sentence.

1. What is the (bases / basis) of your argument?

2. Initials are always written in (capital / capitol) letters.

3. A (byte / bite) is a piece of information made of 8 bits.

4. Did you see today's want (ad / add) for movie extras?

5. The (whether / weather) was so poor we couldn't ski.

6. I ordered a big bowl of (chilly / chili) con carne.

7. It is against his (principals / principles) to lie or cheat.

8. She searched in (vain / vein) for her missing diary.

B To learn the two-word answer to the question in the box, fill in the blanks with words that match the definitions.

> **PROOFREADING CAREFULLY + CHECKING THE DICTIONARY = ?**

1. _A_ __ __ ☐ __ __ __ __
2. _A_ __ ☐ __ __ __ __ __ __
3. _M_ __ __ ☐ __
4. _E_ __ ☐ __ __ __ __
5. _Z_ __ ☐ __ __ __
6. _M_ __ ☐ __ __
7. _I_ __ __ ☐ __ __ __
8. _T_ __ __ __ __ __ ☐ __

CLUES:
1. name unknown; *an ___ writer*
2. a teenager
3. digs for coal or gold
4. physical activity
5. more than one 0
6. person under 21
7. to break in or cut off
8. large land turtle

100

C Find the misspelled word. Rewrite the sentence correctly.

1. Don't withold your help when someone needs it.

_____

2. This school's curiculum offers a variety of classes.

_____

3. Their house was wholely destroyed in the fire.

_____

4. Everyone loves him for his sunny, cheerful temperment.

_____

D Write on the lines the correct spelling of the words in parentheses.

The cold weather was *not* (tipical) _____ for this time of year.
A large (quanity) _____ of (icycles) _____ hung from
the roof. I knew I would be in (jepardy) _____ if I went outside, but
I had no choice. I would *not* miss out this time! I put the (vaccum) _____
cleaner away. Then I put on my coat and (lether) _____ gloves. I
was ready to take care of (busness) _____. It was very difficult to
(manoover) _____ down the sidewalk. Suddenly, I fell, biting my
(toungue) _____ as I landed. It throbbed with a painful (rythm)
_____. It took all my (strenth) _____ to continue. Surely,
no one else would be out on a day like this. But when I finally reached my
destination. There I saw not a ticket line, but only a (boquet) _____
of (butifull) _____ flowers leaning against the "Sold Out" sign.
Once again, there would be no Rolling Stones concert for me.

MY PERSONAL SPELLING DEMONS

List all the words that you misspell more than once. Use your best handwriting and arrange the words in alphabetical order. Keep this list handy for quick reference.

WORD LIST

A
absence
accessible
accommodate
accuracy
accuse
achieve
acknowledge
acquaint
across
aggression
aisle
always
amateur
annually
anonymous
apparent
aquarium
asphalt
assistance
athlete
attendance
attorney
authority
awfully

B
badge
balance
ballet
bargain
basically
beauty
behavior
believe
benefit
biscuit

bookkeeper
boulder
breakfast
breathe
buffet
bulletin
bureaucrat
business
busy

C
cafeteria
calendar
camouflage
campaign
canal
candidate
category
ceiling
certain
changeable
character
children
chocolate
chorus
climb
cocoa
collar
color
colossal
column
committee
complexion
concede
condemn
conscience
conscientious

consequence
contestant
convenient
cooperate
cough
couple
courageous
courtesy
cousin
crescent
criticize
cupboard
curiosity
curriculum

D
dairy
debt
decision
definite
delicious
deodorant
descendant
desirable
despair
desperation
dessert
diamond
dictionary
difference
digestible
dilemma
dining
disappear
disappointment
discipline
disease

dissatisfied
disturb
division
doctor
dollars
driving

E
earring
echoes
effect
efficient
eight
eliminate
embarrass
emergency
emperor
emphasize
endeavor
enough
enthusiastic
environment
equal
escape
especially
exaggerate
exceed
excellent
except
excuse
exercise
exhaust
existence
extension
extraordinary
extremely

F

false
familiarize
fascinate
fashionable
fatigue
favorite
February
feud
fierce
finally
financial
foreign
forfeit
forget
formerly
forty
fountain
fourth
fragile
frantically
fraud
frequent
friend
fuel
fulfill

G

gauge
generally
generous
genius
ghost
goes
gorgeous
government
gracious
graduate
grammar
grateful
grief
grudge
guarantee
guard
guess
guest
guidance

H

half
handkerchief
handsome
harassment
hasten
haven't
having
hazardous
heaven
hedge
height
heir
heredity
heroes
hindrance
hoarse
honorable
horrible
hospital
hour
humorous
hundred
hurriedly
hypothesis

I

icicle
icy
idealize
ideally
identify
ignorant
immature
immediately
incidental
incredible
independence
indispensable
individual
influential
injuries
innocent
instead
institution
insurable
intellectual
intentional
interest
interference
interpret
interrupt
irrelevant
irresistible
irresponsible
island
itemize

J

jealousy
jeopardy
jewelry
jostle
journal
journey
joyous
judge
juice
junior
justice

K

kangaroo
kennel
kept
kitchen
knack
knead
knew
knife
knight
knot
knowledge

L

laboratory
laid
language
laundry
lawyer
lead
league
leather
led
ledge
legislature
legitimate
leisure
library
license
lieutenant

lightning
likable
limousine
liquid
listener
literature
logical
loneliness
loose
losing
loving
loyal
luxury

M

machinery
magician
magnificent
maintain
maintenance
making
manageable
maneuver
mantel
manual
manufacturer
marriage
marshmallow
mathematics
meant
measurement
mechanical
medicine
mediocre
miniature
minute
miscellaneous

mischievous
misspell
moral
mortgage
mosquito
municipal
muscle
musician
mysterious

N

naive
national
naughty
necessarily
negligence
neigh
neighbor
neither
nervous
nickel
niece
ninety
noise
noticeable
nucleus
nudge
nuisance
numb
numerous
nutritious

O

oath
obey
observant
obstacle
occasionally

occurrence
often
omission
once
opinion
opponent
opportunity
opposite
orchestra
ordinary
original
ought
outrageous

P

pageant
paid
pamphlet
panel
parallel
particular
pastime
patient
pedestal
perceive
perform
permanent
persistent
personal
personnel
perspiration
physical
physician
pleasant
politician
possess
possible

potatoes
practically
preference
prejudice
presence
prevalent
principle
privilege
probably
professional
profitable
prominent
pursue

Q

quaint
qualify
quantity
quarrel
quarter
questionnaire
quietly
quirk
quite

R

raise
realistic
realize
receipt
receive
recent
recognize
recommendation
reference
referred
rehearsal
reign

relieve
remembrance
removable
repetition
require
reservoir
resign
responsibility
restaurant
revolutionary
rhythm
ridiculous
rough
route

S

safety
satellite
Saturday
sauce
scarred
scene
scent
schedule
scientist
secretary
seize
sense
sensible
separation
sergeant
several
shaky
shepherd
shining
signature
similar

sincerely
society
sophisticated
sophomore
spouse
stationery
stomach
straighten
strength
strictly
succeed
sufficient
sugar
summary
supervisor
surprise
susceptible
syllable

T

table
taught
technique
temperature
temptation
tendency
terror
thigh
thoroughly
though/thought
through
throughout
tolerance
tomatoes
tomorrow
tongue
tonight

too
tough
traffic
tragedy
transferred
transparent
traveling
tremendous
trouble
truly
Tuesday
twelfth
two
typical

U

ugly
unanimous
unavoidable
unbelievable
unconscious
undoubtedly
unique
universal
unmistakable
unnatural
unnecessarily
until
unusual
usable
used
useful
usually

V

vaccine
vacuum
vain

vegetable
vehicle
vengeance
view
village
villain
violence
virtue
visible
visitor

W

waist
weather
Wednesday
weight
weird
welcome
whale
whisper
whistle
wholly
withhold
woman
wreath
wrench
wrestle
wrinkle
wrist
writing

Y

yacht
yawn
yolk
youngest

SPELLING REFERENCE GUIDE

❶ Consonants and vowels

Consonants are speech sounds that block or partly block the breath with the tongue, teeth, or lips. All the letters of the alphabet, *except a, e, i, o, u,* and sometimes *y* are consonants.

Vowels are speech sounds made by using the voice without blocking the breath with the tongue, teeth, or lips. The letters that make vowel sounds are *a, e, i, o, u,* and sometimes *y.*

❷ Consonant clusters

Consonant clusters are groups of two or more letters that make a single sound. Consonant clusters appear in many English words.

ri**ch**, pa**tch**, **wh**ere, **sh**ed, so**ng**

❸ Short vowels

Short vowel sounds are made with a quick flow of breath.

c**a**p, s**e**t, n**i**p, h**o**p, c**u**p

❹ Long vowels

Long vowel sounds are the same as the name of the letter. These sounds are made with a longer flow of breath.

c**a**ke, m**ee**t, k**i**te, h**o**pe, m**u**le, cr**y**

❺ Long *a* sound

Long *a* may be spelled *a, ai,* or *ei.*

f**a**de, g**ai**n, **ei**ghty

❻ Long *e* sound

Long *e* may be spelled *e, ea, ee, ei, ie,* or *y.*

b**e**cause, t**ea**m, w**ee**p, dec**ei**ve, th**ie**f, onl**y**

❼ Long *i* sound

Long *i* may be spelled *i, ie, igh,* or *y.*

r**i**pe, p**ie**, f**igh**t, fr**y**

❽ Long *o* sound

Long *o* may be spelled *o, oa, ow,* or *ough.*

t**o**ne, b**oa**t, gl**ow**, d**ough**

❾ Long *u* sound

Long *u* may be spelled *u, eu, ew, iew, o, oo, ou, ue,* or *ui.*

c**u**te, f**eu**d, st**ew**, v**iew**, d**o**, t**oo**l, s**ou**p, gl**ue**, br**ui**se

❿ Homophones

Homophones are words that sound alike but have different meanings and different spellings. A mistakenly chosen homophone appears to be a spelling error.

die/dye   for/four   which/witch   your/you're

⓫ Prefixes

A prefix is one or more syllables joined to the beginning of a base word or root to change its meaning. The spelling of a word does not change when a prefix is added.

PREFIX	MEANING	EXAMPLES
un	not	*uneventful unlimited*
in	not	*ineffective inactive*
il	not	*illegible illogical*
im	not	*improper immature*
ir	not	*irreversible irresistible*
de	off, away from	*deport deemphasize*
dis	away from, out of	*discharge disgrace*
mis	wrong, wrongly	*misunderstand mispronounce*
inter	among, between	*interview interact*
sub	under, less than	*subtract submerge*
per	through, by	*perforate perjure*
pro	before, favoring	*proclaim pronounce*
pre	before, ahead	*preheat predict*

Dozens of additional prefixes are used in hundreds of words. Some of these prefixes are *anti, auto, cent, tele, tri, under, semi, mono, uni, kilo, milli, mega, micro, hypo,* and *hyper.*

12 Suffixes

A suffix is a syllable or group of syllables added to the end of a base word or root to change its meaning. Some suffixes change the spelling of the original word.

13 Suffix: *ly*

The suffix *ly* makes an adverb of an adjective.

> slow**ly**, kind**ly**, quick**ly**

14 Suffixes: *ful, less*

You will not usually change a word's spelling when you add *ful* or *less*.

> dread**ful**, care**ful**
> sense**less**, care**less**

If the base word ends in *y*, however, change the *y* to *i* before adding *ful* or *less*.

> dut**iful**, beaut**iful**   penn**iless**, merc**iless**

15 Suffixes: *ise, ize*

These suffixes turn nouns into verbs. Although there are no rules to help you decide between these spellings, many more words end in *ize* than *ise*.

> advert**ise**   memor**ize**

16 Suffixes: *ant, ance, ancy, ent, ence, ency*

These suffixes turn verbs into nouns. There are no rules to help you choose between the *a* or *e* spellings. As with other suffixes, however, you must first drop the base word's final *e* or change the final *y* to *i*.

> pleas**ant**, signific**ance**, tru**ancy**,
> excell**ent**, pati**ence**, emerg**ency**

17 Suffixes: *ed, t, ing*

The word endings *ed* and *t* show the past tense form of a verb. The *ing* ending shows ongoing action in the present. Only a few verbs form the past tense with *t*.

> mean**t**, slep**t**

Drop the verb's final *e* before adding *ed* or *ing*.

> smil**ed**, smil**ing**

Usually, if the verb ends in *y*, change the *y* to *i* before adding *ed*. Do *not* change the *y* before adding *ing*.

> worri**ed**, worry**ing** (Exceptions are words like *played, enjoyed, stayed*.)

18 Suffix: *ous*

This suffix turns a noun into an adjective. In most words, the noun's spelling does not change.

> poison**ous**, mountain**ous**

If the noun ends in *f*, however, change the *f* to *v* before adding *ous*.

> mischie**vous**, grie**vous**

Usually, you will drop a noun's final *e* before adding *ous*.

> ridicul**ous**, nerv**ous**

If the noun ends in *ge*, however, you will *not* drop the *e*.

> courage**ous**, outrage**ous**

If the noun ends in *ce*, change the *e* to *i* before adding *ous*.

> graci**ous**, spaci**ous**

19 Suffixes: *er, est*

These suffixes make comparisons when added to adjectives or adverbs. They show *more* and *most*.

> small**er**, small**est**   rich**er**, rich**est**

As you do before adding other suffixes, first change the base word's *y* to *i*.

> friendli**er**, friendli**est**   angri**er**, angri**est**

20 Suffixes: *tion, sion*

These word endings turn verbs into nouns. Before adding these suffixes, you will often change the spelling of the base word.

If the base word ends in *se* or *te*, drop the *e* before adding *tion*.

> educate/educa**tion**   tense/ten**sion**

If the base word ends in *ce*, drop the *e* before adding *tion*.

> produce/produc**tion**   deduce/deduc**tion**

If the base word ends in *t*, add *ion*.

act/action   reflect/reflection

If the base word ends in *ss*, add *ion*.

confess/confession   aggress/aggression

If the base word ends in *d* or *de*, drop the *d* or *de* and add *sion*.

conclude/conclusion   extend/extension

Some base words end in *a__e* or *i__e*. With these words, you drop the *e* and add *ation*.

separate/separation   organize/organization

㉑ Suffixes: *ary, ery*

Only a few words end in *ery*.

cemetery, very, stationery

To be certain, you should always check a dictionary. But most words that end in this sound contain the *ary* spelling.

secretary, necessary, temporary

㉒ Suffixes: *able, ible*

A noun that ends in *ation* becomes an adjective when you add *able*.

**demonstration/demonstrable
explanation/explainable**

A noun that ends in *ion* becomes an adjective with *ible*.

**division/divisible
comprehension/comprehensible**

The letters *ss* are usually followed by *ible*.

permissible, admissible

Although many more words end in *able* than *ible*, it is always best to check a dictionary.

㉓ Suffixes: *er, or, ian*

These three suffixes name a person who *does* something. Some change verbs into nouns. Usually, the spelling of the base word does not change.

player, doctor, musician

If the verb ends in *e*, drop the final *e* before adding *er*.

writer, faker, biker

Dozens of additional suffixes are used in many hundreds of words. Some of these suffixes are *ist, ism, ity, itis, like, mony, ose, phobia, ology,* and *ward*.

㉔ Words with *ie/ei*

The old rule for deciding which letter comes first will usually be helpful:

I before *e* except after *c*, or when sounded like *a* as in neighbor or weigh.

thief, belief, receive, receipt, eight, veil

When the *c* is pronounced *sh*, however, it may be followed by *ie*.

efficient, conscience

㉕ Regular and Irregular Plurals

Singular nouns are made plural to show more than one. Usually, a noun is made plural when *s* is added.

toys, boats, governments

Nouns that end in *s, ss, sh, x, ch,* or *z* are made plural by adding *es*.

gases, glasses, dishes, bunches, taxes, buzzes

Some nouns that end in the long *o* sound are made plural by adding *es*.

potatoes, torpedoes

But other nouns that end in long *o* are made plural by adding only an *s*. To be sure, check a dictionary.

pianos, rodeos

Nouns that end in *f* or *fe* are made plural by dropping the *f* or *fe* and adding *ves*.

**knife/knives   loaf/loaves   shelf/shelves
Some exceptions to this rule are *roofs, chiefs, beliefs, staffs.***

Nouns that end in *y* are made plural in two ways. If the letter before the *y* is a consonant, drop the *y* and add *ies*.

city/cities   penny/pennies   story/stories

If the letter before the *y* is a vowel, just add *s*.

trolleys, trays, journeys

Some irregular plurals are *teeth, feet, men, women, children, mice,* and *sheep*.

㉖ The *aw* Sound

This sound can be spelled *a, o, au,* or *aw.*

b**a**ll, **o**ff, ca**u**se, p**aw**

㉗ The *air* Sound

This sound can be spelled *ar, er, air, are,* or *ear.*

area, v**er**y, ch**air**, sh**are**, b**ear**

㉘ The *uh* Sound

This sound can be spelled with any of the five vowels.

alive, oft**e**n, magn**i**fy, at**o**m, h**u**m

㉙ The *uhl* Sound

This sound can be spelled *le, al,* or *el.*

need**le**, loy**al**, lev**el**

㉚ The *ur* Sound

This sound can be spelled *ur, er, ir, or,* or *ar.*

b**ur**n, f**er**n, g**ir**l, w**or**k, sug**ar**

㉛ The *oi* Sound

This sound can be spelled *oy* or *oi.*

t**oy**, c**oi**n

㉜ The *ow* Sound

This sound can be spelled *ow* or *ou.*

g**ow**n, cl**ou**d

㉝ The *oo* Sound

This sound can be spelled *oo, u,* or *ou.*

st**oo**d, f**u**ll, c**ou**ld

㉞ Words with *ough*

This confusing spelling is pronounced in six different ways. Always use a dictionary to doublecheck words with this spelling.

r**ough**, thr**ough**, thor**ough**, b**ough**, d**ough**, b**ough**t

㉟ Words with *augh, igh*

The *augh* spelling is pronounced *aw.* The *igh* spelling is pronounced with the long *i* sound.

t**augh**t, s**igh**t

㊱ Words with *cede, ceed, sede*

These letter combinations are all pronounced *seed.*

pro**ceed**, re**cede**, super**sede**

㊲ Words with *qu*

The *qu* spelling is pronounced *kw.*

queen, **qu**iet, s**qu**int

㊳ Words with *ch, tch*

Both spellings make the *ch* sound you hear in *chop.* After a long vowel sound, use *ch.* After a short vowel sound, use *tch.*

pea**ch**, coa**ch**   ba**tch**, fe**tch**

After a consonant, use *ch.*

in**ch**, lun**ch**

At the beginning of a word, always use *ch.*

champion, **ch**allenge

㊴ Words with *j, g, ge, dge*

The *j* sound in *joy* can be spelled in all four ways. Before the vowels *a, o,* and *u,* use the *j* spelling.

jam, **j**ob, **j**uice

At the end of a word, the *j* sound is almost always spelled *ge* or *dge.* Use *ge* after a long vowel sound or a consonant. Use *dge* after a short vowel sound.

a**ge**, hu**ge**   ju**dge**, e**dge**

㊵ Words with *ph*

In some words the *f* sound is made with the letters *ph.* There are no rules to help you with this spelling. You will have to check a dictionary if you're not sure.

gra**ph**ic, paragra**ph**, telepho**ne**

㊶ Silent Letters: *l, k, b, w, h*

Silent *l* is usually followed by a consonant. Silent *k* nearly always comes at the beginning of a word and is usually followed by *n.* Silent *b* most often comes after *m* or before *t.* Silent *w* usually comes at the beginning of a word and is followed by *h* or *r.* Silent *h* appears at the beginning of a word or after a consonant.

fo**l**k, **k**nock, lam**b**, **w**ring, **h**our, g**h**oul

42. Silent Letters: *c, n, e, t, g*

Silent *c* usually follows *s*. Silent *n* always appears after *m*. Silent *e* usually appears at the end of a word that has a long vowel sound. Silent *t* usually follows *f* or *s*. Silent *g* most often appears before *n*.

science, autum**n**, bik**e**, hus**t**le, champa**g**ne

43. *C* with the Sound of *s/k*

Usually, the *s* sound in a word is spelled *s*. But the *s* sound may be spelled with either an *s* or a *c* when it appears before *e, i,* or *y*. After a long vowel sound, the *s* sound is spelled with *c*.

inno**c**ent, in**c**ident   spi**c**e, tra**c**e

Most often, the *k* sound in a word is spelled *k* or *ck*. But there are many words in which *c* makes the *k* sound.

criminal, mi**c**rophone, ta**c**ti**c**s, **c**olor

Check a dictionary if you're not sure how to spell the *k* sound in a word.

44. The Apostrophe

An apostrophe followed by *s* is used to show ownership or possession with singular nouns.

Tanya**'s** dress   student**'s** locker

An apostrophe is used to show the plurals of letters, numbers, symbols, abbreviations, and words used as illustrations.

A**'s** 9**'s** &**'s** Ph.D.**'s** and**'s** and but**'s**

With plural nouns that end in *s*, ownership or possession is shown by placing the apostrophe after the *s*.

delegates**'** votes   contestants**'** prizes

An apostrophe is used to show where one or more letters have been omitted in a contraction.

we**'ve** they**'d** I**'ll**

An apostrophe is used to show where numbers have been omitted.

the roaring **'**20's   the **'**99 Cadillac

45. Abbreviations

Abbreviations are short ways of writing words or phrases. Abbreviations are used to save time, space, and energy. Most abbreviations are followed by a period.

Market **St.**   **Mrs.** Perez   10 **P.M.**

Some common abbreviations are *not* punctuated with periods.

UN   **mph**   **USA**

Official U.S. postal abbreviations are used for the 50 states. Each of these abbreviations is spelled with two capital letters without final periods.

NY   **CA**   **IL**

46. The Hyphen

A hyphen is used in compound numbers from 21 to 99.

twenty-one   forty-seven

A hyphen is used in fractions used as adjectives.

two-thirds majority   **one-half** interest

A hyphen always follows the prefixes *self, ex,* and *all*.

All-American   **self**-respect   **ex**-convict

A hyphen is always used with prefixes before a proper noun, a proper adjective, or the name of an office.

mid-July   **pro**-Israeli   **ex**-governor

Hyphens are used to connect some compound words.

sister-in-law   **great-grandmother**
long-winded   **open-minded**